Praise for
Take the Day Off

"Robert Morris is one of the most uniquely gifted men I have met. His writings have left a profound impact on the church at large, and Gateway Church is making its mark on the course of church history. With all the skills and gifts that could be mentioned as the cause for his profound impact, he gives us a glimpse into the surprising secret behind it all. His life is one of rest. His inner world is flourishing because he has found the rhythm of God for his life, and out of that rhythm flows radical generosity. I strongly encourage every believer to read and reread this book. I pray it becomes a staple in every Christian home, where we function at our highest level, and can, in turn, raise a generation to do the same. It's time to find the rhythm of God for ourselves and impact the world around us for the glory of God."

—Bill Johnson, senior leader at Bethel Church in Redding, California, and author of *The Way of Life* and *Raising Giant-Killers*

"TAKE THE DAY OFF is a timely book that will truly help us understand God's will for our lives in the area of rest. This book will show you why it's important to rest, how it's beneficial to every area of your life, and why it's such a big deal to God. I'm thankful for Pastor Robert's leadership, his ministry, and his example, and I continue to be inspired by his voice."

—Chad Veach, lead pastor of Zoe Church and author of *Unreasonable Hope* and *Faith Forward Future*

"As I work with CEOs and other high performers, overload is one of their biggest issues. The boundaries of time and space have disappeared and now anyone (including bosses) can find you anytime and anywhere. You are never safe until you remember that God has commanded us to protect some time to rest. Neuroscience and other fields have proven it to be true, and Robert gives us some practical ways to do it. Thank you, Robert, for this admonishment!"

—Dr. Henry Cloud, psychologist and
coauthor of *Boundaries*

"I discovered a deep revelation of the importance of Sabbath from Pastor Robert's teaching years ago. Applying these principles of rest to my life has greatly impacted me and my family and has allowed us to run the marathon of life well. I encourage you to read and apply the wisdom of this book to your life!"

—Kari Jobe Carnes, worship leader and songwriter

Take the Day Off

RECEIVING GOD'S GIFT OF REST

ROBERT MORRIS

Faith
Words

NASHVILLE   NEW YORK

FaithWords
Hachette Book Group
1290 Avenue of the Americas, New York, NY 10104
faithwords.com
twitter.com/faithwords

First Edition: October 2019

FaithWords is a division of Hachette Book Group, Inc. The FaithWords name and logo are trademarks of Hachette Book Group, Inc.

The publisher is not responsible for websites (or their content) that are not owned by the publisher.

The Hachette Speakers Bureau provides a wide range of authors for speaking events. To find out more, go to www.hachettespeakersbureau.com or call (866) 376-6591.

Additional copyright information is on page 217.

Library of Congress Control Number:2019944331

ISBNs: 978-1-5460-1016-6 (hardcover), 978-1-5460-1014-2 (ebook)

Printed in the United States of America

LSC-C

10 9 8 7 6 5 4 3 2 1

This book is dedicated to the Lord, who in His infinite love and care for us, created a seven-day week, just so we could rest one day every week and "Take the Day Off!"

ACKNOWLEDGMENTS

I want to thank the members and elders of Gateway Church, who walk in these principles and understand how important it is for me to walk in them also.

I want to thank David Holland, my writing partner for this book and many others. He helps me take the truths that God gives me and express them in written form. He is truly a great man of God, a theologian in his own right, gifted by God, and has worked very hard to develop his writing skill to an excellent and incredible level. Only eternity will tell how many people he has helped understand God and His ways better.

CONTENTS

FOREWORD BY MAX LUCADO

Sheep can't sleep. Perhaps the reason we count sheep to help us sleep is because they are awake.

Sheep struggle to calm down. It's understandable. They are defenseless. They have no sharp teeth or claws. They run slow. When they fall over, they struggle to stand up. They cannot protect themselves. Consequently, they are hesitant to relax.

For sheep to sleep, everything must be just right. No predators. No tension in the flock. No bugs in the air. No hunger in the belly. Everything has to be just so. Unfortunately the sheep cannot find safe pasture, nor can they spray insecticide, deal with the frictions, or find food. They need help. They need a shepherd to help them "lie down in green pastures" (Ps. 23:2). Without a shepherd, they can't rest.

Without a shepherd, neither can we.

We work hard. There is money to be made. There are degrees to be earned. There are ladders to be climbed. Busyness is next to godliness. We idolize Thomas Edison who claimed he could exist on fifteen-minute naps. (Somehow we forget to mention Albert Einstein who averaged eleven hours of sleep a night.) In 1910 Americans slept 9 hours a night, today we sleep 7 and are proud of it. And we are tired because of it. Our minds are tired. Our bodies are tired. But much more importantly, our souls are tired.

We are eternal creatures and we ask eternal questions. From where did I come? To where am I going? What is right? What is wrong? When I've done wrong, how can I be made right? Do I have a Maker and does my Maker care about me? These are the primeval questions of the soul. And these are the kind of questions which, left unanswered, will steal our sleep.

Yet we are so busy making a living, we have no time to ponder the meaning of living.

Our Good Shepherd has a better idea. "He makes me to lie down" (Ps. 23:2). The One who leads us has a plan to restore us. That plan includes ordained moments of rest. That plan includes a Sabbath day.

It is time to rest. In this powerful, restorative book, Robert Morris calls us back to the ancient practice of regular renewal. I love Robert. He is a dear friend, generous with his wisdom and gracious with his leadership. God has given him a message for our generation. This book will bless you. Read it, then read it again.

A century ago Charles Spurgeon gave this advice to his preaching students:

> Even beasts of burden must be turned out to grass occasionally; the very sea pauses at ebb and flood; earth keeps the Sabbath of the wintry months; and man, even when exalted to God's ambassador, must rest or faint, must trim his lamp or let it burn low; must recruit his vigor or grow prematurely old...In the long run we shall do more by sometimes doing less.[1]

---

1. Helmut Thielicke, *Encounter with Spurgeon*, trans. John W. Doberstein (Philadelphia: Fortress Press, 1963; reprint, Grand Rapids, Mich.: Baker Book House, 1975), 220 (page citation is to the reprint edition).

The bow cannot always be bent without fear of breaking. For a field to bear fruit it must lie fallow. And for you to be healthy, you must rest. Slow down and God will heal you. He will bring rest to your mind, to your body, and most of all, to your soul. He will lead you to green pastures.

START HERE!

What does it take to reduce a grown man—the respected head of a large and rapidly growing enterprise with scores of employees, no less—to a weepy, bewildered, half-dressed heap on his closet floor? Surprisingly little, it turns out, under the right circumstances. "How little," you ask? One morning several years ago, I discovered that nothing more challenging than an empty sock drawer was sufficient to push me over the edge.

That's right. I am that man.

At the time, Gateway Church, the church in the Dallas–Fort Worth metropolitan area it is my privilege to pastor, had been in hyper-growth mode for years. We'd all pretty much been charging forward at a dead run from the day we founded the church with only a small group of friends in a living room, but me most of all. In the early days of any church startup, the founder is not only the preacher, but also the business manager, operations manager, personnel director, and the custodian.

Growth brought help and increased division of labor, but the pressures and demands expanded in parallel. A second Sunday morning service was added, followed by a Saturday night service. Then came more services on both days. Within a few years I found myself preaching five or six times each weekend and leading a large, seemingly ever-growing staff during the week.

At the same time, the increased profile of the church and some well-received books resulted in a steady stream of invitations to speak across North America and around the world. I felt obligated to say yes to as many of these as I could. "After all," I reasoned, "surely the invitation wouldn't have come my way if God didn't want me to go help those people." I presumed, often without asking, that every invitation was an expression of God's favor and blessing. And that as a good steward, I was obligated to take on everything that came my way. Of course, I was also fully committed to being the best husband and father I could be. Indeed, my heart, value system, and biblical beliefs all demanded that I put family first. So, I had been striving mightily to live out that conviction. But I had been running on empty for years and it was finally catching up with me—physically, mentally, and emotionally.

I wasn't the only one in our household stretched increasingly thin. As the church grew, my wife Debbie found herself with more to do and more places to be. As it happens, my "hitting the wall" moment happened to coincide with her being out of town for a week at a women's conference.

On one fateful morning in the middle of that week, I dragged myself out of bed early, my mind already whirling with the multitude of things I needed to accomplish that day, and the precious, limited time available for those tasks in between multiple meetings. Every item on my mental to-do list seemed important. So did the meetings that increasingly crowded my schedule. My practical instinct was to try to prioritize, but everything shouted with equal urgency. Everything seemed to vie for the label "Top Priority."

> Every item on my mental to-do list seemed important.

After a quick shower, I headed to get dressed, opened my underwear drawer in the chest in my closet, and was greeted by a terrifying sight.

I was down to may last pair of clean underwear.

A surge of alarm hit me. *What will I do tomorrow? There's no more underwear!?* As I pulled the last remaining pair on, I pulled myself together by assuring myself that I would figure something out later. After all, I had a whole twenty-four hours to solve this crisis.

Then I opened my sock drawer. My *empty* sock drawer.

I know it seems ridiculous, but that was it. That was the grain of sand that tipped the scales of my fragile physical and emotional well-being. That was the flimsy little hay straw that proved too much for the staggering camel. Sometimes after months of silent snowfall, a single snap of a twig is all it takes to trigger the avalanche that roars down the mountainside. The tiny issue of "no clean socks" was that twig snap. A wave of deep sadness washed over me. I dropped to the floor and began to weep.

Don't judge me. I was perfectly capable of running a load of laundry. I was licensed and duly authorized by Debbie to operate our Maytag front loader. Or, alternatively, as a functioning adult in possession of a wallet containing cash, I was quite capable of stopping at Target or Walmart on the way to the office and purchasing socks and underwear with my own money. There were numerous easy solutions to this problem, but in that particular moment I was incapable of bringing any of them to my consciousness. Any solution, no matter how simple, constituted "one more thing to do." My overburdened mind and under-rested soul were simply too weary to choose one. I was essentially frozen in fatigue.

Today I can laugh about the Great Underwear Crisis of 2005. It truly is absurd. I eventually pulled myself together, fished a matching (I think) pair of socks out of the dirty clothes hamper, and got on with my day. I was only lost in despair for a moment, but it was a frightening moment. So when I arrived at the office, I took the first opportunity I had to confide in our senior executive pastor, Tom Lane. Tom was and is a wise elder counselor and friend. He'd been supporting and serving senior pastors for about as long as I'd been a Christian. After describing my meltdown that morning, I finished with the question that had been haunting me all morning: "Tom, am I losing it?"

He smiled and said, "No, Robert, you're just exhausted. You've been pushing too hard for too long. You just need some real, deep rest." And he was right. I had become just another victim of the great silent epidemic of our times.

Epidemic is a strong word, but it's the appropriate one here. Precisely one hundred years ago another kind of scourge was sweeping the world and killing millions. Between 1918 and 1920, roughly five hundred million people were infected by the Spanish Flu and somewhere between fifty million and one hundred million died around the world. In the United States, it's estimated that 28 percent of the population eventually became infected and somewhere between 500,000 and 675,000 Americans died.

At the height of the epidemic, many Americans opened their morning paper each day and found two lists of names on the front page. The shorter of the two lists contained the names of local servicemen who had been killed in World War I. A longer list held the names of those who had died of the Spanish flu.

Thankfully, in the century since those terrifying days, science and technology have gone a long way toward eliminating those kinds of appalling death tolls by disease. But that progress has come at a price. The rise of modern technology has been a double-edged sword—accelerating the pace of life, extending our workdays, and breaking down the barriers between workplace and home.

All of the Western world experienced these changes, but America's unique culture amplified them. We're a nation built upon the ideas of freedom, individualism, and achievement. With God's providential help, the founders created a dynamic place where class or station at birth meant almost nothing. Anyone willing to work hard, sacrifice, and apply themselves could achieve anything. The US became a magnet for the destitute and downtrodden of the world not because of its social welfare safety net. (There wasn't one.) America became the promised land because a person could arrive penniless and through diligence, thrift, talent, and ambition become virtually anything they could imagine.

Yes, any person could go as far as their energy, creativity, and diligence could carry them. That's the heart of the miraculous American dream. It's a wondrous thing. But along the way during these last hundred years, we laid something aside that those previous generations of Americans understood and held sacred. Something that made living "the good life" possible. We'll identify and explore that lost "something" in great detail on the pages that follow. For now, just know that its abandonment has unleashed another kind of epidemic across our land.

That's right; today our culture of self-improvement and self-advancement through individual effort has resulted in tens of millions living burned-out, stressed-out lives. We're never off and never unplugged. We're never quiet. We're never *not* bombarded by tasks, information, obligations, stimulations, and aggravations. And it's taking an enormous toll on our well-being. It's a plague of spirit, soul, and body exhaustion.

> We're never off and never unplugged. We're never quiet.

It's not just us adults who are suffering the devastating effects of this twenty-first-century pandemic. Increasingly, even children are falling victim to our culture's obsession with busyness. Shocking numbers of teens and preteens are over-scheduled, overcommitted, and under rested. As a result, children too increasingly show all the signs of stress and burnout.

I'm not pointing fingers here. As I've already made clear, I too have fallen victim to the plague of our times. In fact, this epidemic came close to laying me low on more than one occasion before the Lord opened my eyes to the neglected, revolutionary spiritual key I will present to you on the pages that follow. I'm honored and excited to offer you the biblical cure that saved me.

About a quarter century ago, a Christian family physician from Wisconsin named Richard Swenson wrote a timely and insightful book prompted by the steady stream of stressed-out, worn out, burned-out people he kept treating in his office week after week. In *Margin: Restoring Emotional, Physical, Financial, and Time Reserves to Overloaded Lives*, Dr. Swenson diagnosed a single root of much of the sickness and physical breakdown he was being asked to treat in his medical practice. That diagnosis? Too many people living with too little in their lives of something he called "margin." He said most of us are living "marginless" lives. What did Dr. Swenson mean by this? He opened his book by contrasting living *with* margin to living *without* it:

Marginless is being thirty minutes late to the doctor's office because you were twenty minutes late getting out of the bank because you were ten minutes late dropping the kids off at school because the car ran out of gas two blocks from the gas station—and you forgot your wallet. Margin, on the other hand, is having breath left at the top of the staircase, money left at the end of the month, and sanity left at the end of adolescence.

Marginless is the baby crying and the phone ringing at the same time; margin is Grandma taking the baby for the afternoon. Marginless is being asked to carry a load five pounds heavier than you can lift; margin is a friend to carry half the burden. Marginless is not having time to finish the book you're reading on stress. Margin is having the time to read it twice.[1]

Think about this: If marginless living—and the physical, mental, emotional, and financial toll that comes with it—was a significant problem back in the midnineties, it is surely far, far worse today. Dr. Swenson's book was published back when email and the internet were only embryonic novelties, phones were "mobile" but not "smart," and the future founders of Facebook, Twitter, and Instagram were all prepubescent kids in their bedrooms playing *Super Mario Kart* on Super Nintendo game consoles. The dizzying technological changes that have emerged over the last two decades have served only to crowd, hurry, and busy our lives even more. Today, a wide range of authorities are sounding the alarm about

1. Richard A. Swenson, *Margin: Restoring Emotional, Physical, Financial, and Time Reserves to Overloaded Lives*, Kindle ed. (Colorado Springs: NavPress, 2002), 13.

both the physical and mental toll our epidemic of marginlessness is taking on us as a people.

On the medical front for example, a 2017 piece for CNN titled "Stress Really Is Killing Us" reported, "Stress-related disorders and diseases have been on the rise in the whole population for decades, according to data from the Centers for Disease Control and Prevention."[2] Along the same lines, a 2016 study measured what it called the "physiological stress load" of Americans of all races and income levels. It found that health indicators tied to heart, kidney, and liver disease were closely tied to levels of stress. It also found that the stress load of the average American has been rapidly increasing since the late 1970s.[3] According to one expert on balancing work and life, "Stress is a factor in five out of the six leading causes of death—heart disease, cancer, stroke, lower respiratory disease, and accidents. An estimated 75 percent to 90 percent of all doctor visits are for stress-related issues."[4]

> The stress load of the average American has been rapidly increasing since the late 1970s.

Our increasing lack of margin is damaging more than our bodies, however. As I discovered the hard way, it ravages our minds and emotions as well. A respected online source for mental health

2. Daniel Keating, "Stress Really Is Killing Us," CNN, 2017, https://www.cnn .com/2017/04/02/opinions/stress-killing-us-keating-opinion/index.html.

3. Diane Whitmore Schanzenbach et al., "Money Lightens the Load," Hamil tonProject.org, 2016, http://www.hamiltonproject.org/papers/money_lightens _the_load.

4. Joe Robinson, "Three-Quarters of Your Doctor Bills Are Because of This," HuffingtonPost.com, 2013, https://www.huffingtonpost.com/joe-robinson/stress -and-health_b_3313606.html.

information lists the following as possible warning signs of burnout or emotional exhaustion:[5]

- Sense of failure and self-doubt
- Feeling helpless, trapped, and defeated
- Detachment, feeling alone in the world
- Loss of motivation
- Increasingly cynical and negative outlook
- Decreased satisfaction and sense of accomplishment

Currently, millions upon millions of people in our culture are living daily with these symptoms. Far too many of them are believers. Christian counselor David Murray, author of the book *Reset: Living a Grace-Paced Life in a Burnout Culture*, says we're experiencing "an epidemic of burnout" in the Church.[6] It's certainly true among my fellow pastors. The words "burnout" and "ministry" have become tightly linked.

For many Americans and their doctors, the path to relieving the negative effects of exhaustion and stress seemingly runs through the local pharmacy. A 2013 study revealed that one in every six adult Americans was on some sort of prescribed psychiatric drug like an antianxiety or antidepressant medication.[7] Some unknown but very

---

5. Melinda Smith et al., "Burnout Prevention and Treatment," HelpGuide.org, accessed November 2018, https://www.helpguide.org/articles/stress/burnout -prevention-and-recovery.html/.

6. David Murray, "4 Cultural Factors that Contribute to Our Epidemic of Burnout," Crossway.org, 2017, https://www.crossway.org/articles/4-cultural -factors-that-contribute-to-our-epidemic-of-burnout/.

7. Sara Miller, "1 in 6 Americans Takes a Psychiatric Drug," *Scientific American*, 2016, https://www.scientificamerican.com/article/1-in-6-americans-takes -a-psychiatric-drug/.

large percentage of the individuals taking these medications are likely suffering either the physical or psychological effects of living without margin. They're simply chronically under rested.

The physical, emotional, and mental impacts are troubling enough for any individual. But when you add up the costs across our entire society, it begins to look like a crisis. A 2016 article in *Forbes* magazine attempted to put a price tag on the damage to our economy. The piece cited a study that estimated that "as many as one million people per day miss work because of stress." The cost of this lost productivity was estimated to be between $150 billion and $300 billion annually for American employers.[8]

I know exhaustion certainly represented a crisis for me, as it will for you or someone you love.

So, is there an answer? Is there a cure for this epidemic? I'm happy to report there is. Like most other solutions that actually work, we'll find that it's been hiding in plain sight all along—in our Bibles.

---

8. Ashley Stahl, "Here's What Burnout Costs You," Forbes.com, 2016, https://www.forbes.com/sites/ashleystahl/2016/03/04/heres-what-burnout-costs-you/#318f26ee4e05.

CHAPTER ONE

THE FORGOTTEN COMMANDMENT

We cannot break the commandments, we can only break ourselves against them.

—G.K. Chesterton

Roughly thirty-five centuries ago, a vast multitude of people—perhaps two million in number—were encamped at the base of one of the craggy mountains that dot the desert south and east of modern-day Israel. They were waiting. For what, they weren't quite sure. Their leader had climbed the mountain days ago to meet with the same mysterious God who, fifty days earlier, had miraculously led them out of bondage in Egypt.

The twelve tribes of Israel were about to learn that they, through their representative, Moses, had entered into a sacred covenant with the Most High God. This covenant would set them apart as a unique and special people among all the peoples of the earth. They were becoming a chosen people. But chosen for what, exactly? Chosen to be carriers of a seed. They were picked to become a genetic, prophetic, and cultural vessel that would ultimately bring the Savior of the world into the earth. God had been prophesying about and planning for this seed for a very long time. This future Redeemer was "the seed of the woman" who would one day crush the head of the serpent, promised all the way back in the garden immediately after the Fall.[1] This very same seed was foreseen in the promise to Abraham, the father of the Israelite nation, when God said, "In your seed all nations of the earth shall be blessed."[2]

This seed that the Israelites would carry as a chosen people was none other than the Redeemer who would eventually be born to undo all the devastation that Adam's Fall had unleashed upon the earth. The Fall had separated man from his Creator. The promised seed would reconnect him, but only if this people could survive and remain separated according to God's plan for another 1,500 years.

In other words, the eternal fate of humanity itself hinged on the Israelites' ability to remain a distinct people and a healthy, successful society through the centuries.

Now, a covenant is like a contract, only far more solemn and sacred. When two parties enter into a written contract, both receive a copy so they can remember what has been agreed to. So, Moses ultimately returned from his mountaintop encounter with the Creator carrying two copies of a covenant document—one for the Israelite people and one for God. In this case, each copy of the agreement was a tablet of stone, with writing on both sides. That writing contained ten stipulations, or "commandments."

Remember, God's purpose in creating this covenant was to form a people who could remain distinct, intact, healthy, and thriving for centuries in a fallen, twisted, decaying world. Those commandments were divinely designed to help them do just that. They were the heart of a system—along with the Levitical regulations found

---

1. See Genesis 3:15
2. Genesis 22:18

in Moses' books of Leviticus and Deuteronomy—that would create a unique culture and society. One that could resist being corrupted by the devastating effects of idolatry. One that could keep families intact, bodies and minds healthy, the land productive, and the social fabric strong.

> This covenant was to form a people who could remain distinct, intact, healthy, and thriving for centuries.

Those ten simple covenant stipulations, carved onto those stone tablets by God's own finger, are a truly remarkable set of rules for living. They held in them the wisdom to live a good life and form a strong society. Of course, the Israelite people as a whole never kept those commandments faithfully or completely. Nevertheless, enough people took them seriously enough, often enough, to keep the Jewish people intact and distinct through centuries of invasion, threat, crisis, exile, and return. Long enough for the fullness of time to come for the arrival of that promised seed. And the more closely they adhered to those rules, the better they did as a people.

The first three commandments centered on how the individual was to relate to God. (Don't worship other gods. Don't make graven images. Don't take God's name in vain.) Meanwhile, the final six commandments spoke to how the individual was to relate to other people (Honor your parents. Don't steal. Don't kill. Don't lie. Etc.)

So, that's the first three, and the last six. That adds up to nine commandments. What about the missing fourth commandment? Well, it is something unique. In a sense, in eight simple words it speaks to how the individual is to relate to God, self, and creation all at once: "Remember the Sabbath day, to keep it holy."[3] However, God didn't

---

3. Exodus 20:8

take any chances about His people misunderstanding what remembering and keeping the Sabbath looked like. So, He followed this command with lots of explanation. In fact, Moses directly followed this commandment with more commentary than any of the other nine!

> "Six days you shall labor and do all your work, but the seventh day is the Sabbath of the LORD your God. In it you shall do no work: you, nor your son, nor your daughter, nor your male servant, nor your female servant, nor your cattle, nor your stranger who is within your gates. For in six days the LORD made the heavens and the earth, the sea, and all that is in them, and rested the seventh day. Therefore the LORD blessed the Sabbath day and hallowed it."[4]

Yes, there was (and is) something special about this particular commandment. God included it and emphasized it because it contains a major key to the Israelites' success as a people. So important to Israel's well-being and survival was it, that God established severe penalties for violating it. According to the Mosaic law, violating the Sabbath carried the death penalty. Eleven chapters later in Exodus, here's what we find God saying to Moses:

> "Therefore you are to observe the Sabbath, for it is holy to you. Everyone who profanes it shall surely be put to death; for whoever does any work on it, that person shall be cut off from among his people. For six days work may be done, but on the seventh day there is a Sabbath of complete rest, holy to the LORD; whoever does any work on the Sabbath day shall surely be put to death."[5]

4. Exodus 20:9–11
5. Exodus 31:14–15 NASB

4

But did God really intend this to be enforced? Was He truly serious about making working on the Sabbath day a capital offense? We find our answer in an incident recorded in the book of Numbers:

> One day while the people of Israel were in the wilderness, they discovered a man gathering wood on the Sabbath day. The people who found him doing this took him before Moses, Aaron, and the rest of the community. They held him in custody because they did not know what to do with him. Then the LORD said to Moses, "The man must be put to death! The whole community must stone him outside the camp." So the whole community took the man outside the camp and stoned him to death, just as the LORD had commanded Moses.[6]

Yes, at God's direct instruction, they executed the man for gathering sticks on the Sabbath. Clearly, God was quite serious about refraining from work on the Sabbath. Profaning the Sabbath was indeed one of several of the Levitical laws that carried the death penalty—among them murder, rape, and bestiality. Yes, the Sabbath was serious business to God.

I realize this seems excessively harsh to our modern minds. After all, the man was just gathering firewood, for Pete's sake.

But we have to keep in mind that the laws that Moses delivered to the Israelites were designed for their benefit *and* to assure the success of His grand plan of redemption. Those laws contained principles for remaining healthy as individuals and families, and strong as a society. God understood what we clearly do not. Namely, that a society in which people work seven days a week is just as vulnerable

---

6. 15:32-36 NLT

to collapse as a society in which people are free to rape and murder without consequence. God was crafting a culture and a people that could survive and thrive so that in the fullness of time, His only begotten Son could enter the world through them.

It's very important so I'll say it again. The fate of God's entire plan of redemption for planet Earth rested on forming a unique, resilient, healthy, set-apart people. And clearly, resting one day a week was such a vital key to being such a people, that God made it one of his core, ten stipulations inscribed into his covenant with Israel.

Now, let me ask you a question: If God was this serious about the Sabbath, how serious should we be about it today? Let's dive deeper into God's Word and find out.

A Rest Remains

For me, hitting the wall of exhaustion brought me face-to-face with the vital wisdom principle embedded in the fourth commandment. I'm talking about the principle of rest. This principle is a thread that runs throughout the Bible.

Once you start looking for it, you see it all throughout Scripture, including in the New Testament! It's an eye-opening exercise to explore this truth in our Bibles, so let's begin with the book of Hebrews, a New Testament book devoted almost completely to explaining how the New Covenant relates to the Old. In the fourth chapter there is an entire passage that addresses the principle of rest:

For only we who believe can enter his rest. As for the others, God said, "In my anger I took an oath: 'They will never enter my place of rest,'" even though this rest has been ready since he made the world. We know it is ready because of the place in the Scriptures where it mentions the seventh day: "On the seventh day God rested from all his work." But in the other passage God said, "They will never enter my place of rest."[7]

Here, a New Testament book quotes and references two key Old Testament passages about rest. First, he directs us to Psalm 95:11 ("They will never enter my rest."), then he points us all the way back to the first pages of our Bibles, to the creation account in Genesis Chapter 2 ("On the seventh day God rested from all his work."). Note that God established and modeled the principle of rest right from the very beginning of creation. We'll explore that truth further in a moment.

Notice also how the Holy Spirit-inspired author then goes on to connect these two Old Testament passages to each other:

> So God's rest is there for people to enter, but those who first heard this good news failed to enter because they disobeyed God. So God set another time for entering his rest, and that time is today. God announced this through David much later in the words already quoted: "Today when you hear his voice, don't harden your hearts." Now if Joshua had succeeded in giving them this rest, God would not have spoken about another day of rest still to come. So there is a special rest still waiting for the people of God.[8]

I find this amazing. Right in our New Testament the author of Hebrews declares that a Sabbath rest is "still waiting for the people of God." The New King James Version says, "So there remains a

---

7. Hebrews 4:3–5 NLT
8. Hebrews 4:6–9 NLT

Sabbath rest for the people of God." That's you and me, by the way. That means there currently is a rest that you and I can and should enter. It is an open and standing invitation. But according to this passage, entering that rest is an act of obedience. In other words, we can choose *not* to enter. What kind of obedience is necessary? The author of Hebrews answered that question in the previous chapter by pointing back to the way the children of Israel were called to "believe God" and, in faith, go take possession of the promised land where they could be at rest as a nation. The writer points out that the first generation of freed Israelites refused to do so and, as a result, died in the wilderness. They refused to enter the rest God had prepared and granted them because of unbelief.[9]

The fact is, the principle of rest is a pattern established right from the beginning of creation and it is still in place today. As we've seen, God personally inscribed it into the Ten Commandments. We've also seen that it is revalidated in the New Testament. And although as a pastor I was familiar with the principle, its importance and relevance had not been fully clear to me until I hit that wall of exhaustion I described at the beginning of this book. With the best of intentions, I had allowed my love for people and the demands of leading a church to progressively crowd out any space for real rest in my life. Because I was chronically ignoring the principle of the Sabbath, I couldn't participate in God's divine plan of restoration.

Far too many Christians are making the same terrible mistake. Many do so because they've been taught that nothing in the Old Testament applies to them. Let's examine that assumption.

---

9. See Hebrews 3:19

Law, Grace, & Principles

How should New Covenant believers view and relate to the laws of the Old Covenant? That's a question theologians, pastors, and believers have been wrestling with since the very beginning days of the Church. We see the original apostles grappling with it in the early chapters of the book of Acts. Large sections of Paul's numerous epistles address this issue as well. As I write these words, huge debates about this very question are currently underway in the evangelical world.

Here's good news. The very understanding that we have just explored about *why* God gave the Old Covenant laws—namely, to create a separated, healthy, thriving people who could carry the seed of the Redeemer in this fallen world until His time to come forth finally arrived—gives us the key to understanding how to relate to those laws under the New Covenant.

The New Testament is clear that our eternal salvation, our forgiveness, and our right standing with God are wholly and completely rooted in Jesus' finished work on the cross. We are made righteous with *His* righteousness,[10] which is a good thing because our own righteousness is utterly, pitifully inadequate.

It's one thing to say that, under the New Covenant, keeping the Mosaic laws no longer has anything to do with our salvation and standing with God. (True.) But it's another thing to claim that those laws no longer contain principles for living well, or for living the kind of life that pleases God. (False!)

Put another way, the Old Covenant laws, especially the Ten Commandments, still reflect God's values, character, and wisdom

---

10. See 2 Corinthians 5:21

for living. They are no longer "laws" to be kept, but they are still very much wisdom principles to be heeded. For example, the sixth commandment says, "You shall not murder." Now ask yourself: Has God changed His attitude toward murder now that we're in the New Covenant? Of course not. And ignoring that commandment will not lead to a good, happy life. And it certainly won't result in a life that pleases and glorifies God. The same can be said of each of the other nine commandments. God made the laws in the Old Covenant precisely because He knew they would help Israel succeed. The wisdom those commandments contain didn't evaporate the moment the New Covenant came. Wisdom is still wisdom—even if law keeping is no longer the pathway to a relationship with God.

For example, the law of Moses didn't exist when God was creating the world, yet we find the principle of Sabbath conspicuously present in the Genesis account of creation. In fact, we just saw that Moses' explanation of the fourth commandment pointed back to God's seventh-day rest:

> "For in six days, the Lord made the heavens and the earth, the sea, and all that is in them, and rested the seventh day. Therefore the LORD blessed the Sabbath day and hallowed it."[11]

God Himself rested on the seventh day. In other words, He modeled this principle from the beginning. It's that important. Even so, many (perhaps most) believers assume that because the fourth commandment is in the Old Testament and part of the Mosaic law, that we can freely ignore it. But is that really the case?

I learned the hard way that there are benefits to observing the

---

11. Exodus 20:10–11

principles embedded in the Ten Commandments, and that there are consequences when we do not. Here's a little exercise that should clarify why this is so: I'm going to list several of the other commandments that God gave the people of Israel through Moses. Read each one of the ten and ask yourself two questions: "Are there benefits to incorporating this command into my life?" and, "Are there negative consequences in life if I do not?"

The First Commandment: "You shall have no other gods before me."

As a New Covenant Christian believer in Jesus Christ, are there benefits to not worshipping false gods? Are there negative consequences to living a lifestyle of idolatry? It is indeed possible for a believer to turn their wealth, achievement, status, or any number of other things into an idol. How do things tend to go in life for people who make an idol of anyone or anything? Not well in my experience.

How about the sixth commandment: "You shall not murder"? Again, ask yourself, are there benefits to obeying that commandment? I'm guessing I can put you down as a yes on that one. And are there negative consequences for ignoring it? I'm confident you will agree that there are.

We could run the same exercise with the commandments prohibiting adultery, stealing, lying, and coveting. In each case, nearly all rational Christians would agree that we're better off following these commands from God as wisdom principles—even though they are embedded in the Old Testament. We believe they are fully relevant today, even though, as the Apostle Paul makes clear in the book of Galatians, we're under grace rather than law as far as our standing with God is concerned.

We affirm these other commands without hesitation because we clearly understand that violating them will do harm to ourselves, others, our community, or all three. When you think about it, that's actually the nature of all that God labels "sin." Think about it. Everything the Word of God calls sin is really ultimately harmful to the person who commits it, to someone else, or to the fabric of society. In other words, our wise, loving God's fences and "Keep Out" signs around certain things are entirely for our protection and the protection of those around us.

So why do we exempt the fourth commandment from this logic? *Why do we New Testament Christians still heartily endorse the commandments against murder, adultery, and dishonoring parents, while feeling utterly free from embracing the wisdom of the commandment about resting one day out of seven?*

It seems we often act as if we believe that we should keep nine out of the Ten Commandments. For some reason, the fourth is the only one that we think we can freely ignore without incurring negative consequences for ourselves and others. We say, "That's legalism! That's not for today."

> The wisdom embedded in God's fourth commandment *is* for today.

As I learned, the wisdom embedded in God's fourth commandment *is* for today. That's exactly the point the author of Hebrews was communicating when, on this side of the cross, he wrote: *"Today*, if you will hear His voice, do not harden your hearts."[12]

I had to come to the realization that honoring the Sabbath is on the same list as not killing people. There is no logical or biblical reason to honor one and disregard the other.

Please understand, I'm a grace guy. I love the New Testament's revelation of the grace of God as expressed through His sending of His Son.

12. Hebrews 4:7

Jesus did what we could never do ourselves. He fulfilled all the requirements of the law on our behalf. He lived a life of perfect righteousness and then died in our place on the cross. The result is that those who say yes to His offer of eternal life receive *His* righteousness. As Paul wrote:

> For He made Him who knew no sin to be sin for us, that we might become the righteousness of God in Him.[13]

This is such an important thing to understand! Our right standing with God is wholly and utterly based upon the reality that, as born-again believers, we stand in Jesus' righteousness, not our own. Isaiah reminds us that our own best efforts at righteous living are as filthy, smelly rags[14] in relation to the level of righteousness required to stand before a holy, perfect God. We have eternal life, acceptance, and connection to God solely because Jesus' perfect righteousness has been both imputed and imparted to us.[15]

However, the very real truth that law keeping does not and cannot save us, does not negate the wisdom embedded in the Ten Commandments, or in other aspects of the Old Covenant system such as the principle of "firstfruits." (I dealt with the powerful principle of firstfruits at length in my previous books, *The Blessed Life* and *Beyond Blessed*.)

The wisdom contained in the Old Testament laws didn't suddenly stop being wisdom the weekend Jesus died on the cross and rose from the dead. In fact, the prophet Jeremiah got a prophetic glimpse of the New Covenant that Jesus would institute and wrote this:

---

13. 2 Corinthians 5:21
14. See Isaiah 64:6
15. See Philippians 3:9

"Behold, the days are coming, says the LORD, when I will make a new covenant with the house of Israel and with the house of Judah...But this is the covenant that I will make with the house of Israel after those days, says the LORD: *I will put My law in their minds, and write it on their hearts*; and I will be their God, and they shall be My people."[16] (emphasis added)

Over in the New Testament, Hebrews 10:16 quotes this prophecy and affirms that the Christian faith is indeed that New Covenant that Jeremiah foresaw. The miracle of the new birth does several extraordinary things inside each person who says yes to God's gracious offer of salvation in His Son. It makes a formerly dead spirit alive with the life of God. It cleanses the conscience. It imparts a spirit of adoption by which the heart begins to recognize that God is a person's loving Father. Yet it does something additional. Something very important. The new birth *writes God's law on our hearts.*

You, the believer, no longer need to refer to tablets of stone. The things that please God are encoded right into your inner being. Those laws aren't about trying to earn God's love or favor. The Spirit of God didn't write them on your heart so you could try to be "good" enough to merit some blessings from God. No, they are about living a life of maximum impact for God's kingdom. A good life. A healthy life. A life that shines in a dark and hopeless world so others can be drawn to your light.

Rest Is a Step of Faith

As the author of Hebrews reminded us, honoring the principle of the Sabbath takes faith. It's true. When I talk to Christians about unplug-

---

16. Jeremiah 31:31–33

ging for a full day each week, what I often see in their faces is fear and/or disbelief. I can almost see the thoughts racing through their minds: *Are you kidding me? I can't just do nothing for one day a week. I have too much to do. Too many people are depending on me. Everything will fall to pieces!* I recognize that kind of thinking because I had those same thoughts.

This fear response is very similar to what I encounter in Christians when I present the biblical truth about tithing. Many see it in the Word of God but are frozen by thoughts like: *I can't afford to tithe. I'm barely making it as it is!* If you've read my previous book, *Beyond Blessed*, or its predecessor, *The Blessed Life*, then you already know how I respond to those objections. I and millions of others have learned that I can live much better on 90 percent of my income that has God's blessing on it, than on 100 percent with no blessing on it at all. Tithing requires faith in God's power, ability, and faithfulness to respond with supernatural blessing to my willingness to put Him first in my finances. In the very same way, honoring the principle of the Sabbath requires faith in Him to do the same thing when I follow His principles with my time.

Whereas the promised land was an actual physical territory that God pledged to the people of Israel, our place of rest includes but transcends the physical. Yes, we are called to rest physically, but God also calls us to rest spiritually, emotionally, and mentally. Honoring the principle of the Sabbath reveals a deep level of trust in God—trust that He will empower us to accomplish all that He has called us to do in six days a week, because we've been obedient to be still for one.

Now, if the thought of taking a day off causes you more stress and worry, you're missing the principle of rest. It's not a law that you have to follow. It's about coming to a place of faith and trust that God is our provider and we can live a *lifestyle* of rest! No worry, no anxiety, no fear, and no hurried schedules. Not just a day of rest, but an attitude of rest that permeates every day, every week, all year long!

Rest is a step of obedience through faith.

The writer of Hebrews seems to acknowledge that this is not an easy thing to do. After pointing out that rest is a step of obedience through faith, he says we have to be intentional about resting. In the eleventh verse of chapter four he writes:

Let us therefore be diligent to enter that rest, lest anyone fall according to the same example of disobedience.

The Amplified Bible nicely unpacks the meaning of this exhortation:

Let us therefore be zealous and exert ourselves and strive diligently to enter that rest [of God, to know and experience it for ourselves], that no one may fall or perish by the same kind of unbelief and disobedience [into which those in the wilderness fell].[17]

Why is diligence required to enter into the true Sabbath rest that is so important to God? Because the enemy of your soul and everything in our fallen, natural world is trying to keep you from entering that rest. And if they fail, they will try to pull you out of that position of rest if they can. My near collapse offers a clear illustration of why this is so. Exhaustion came close to destroying everything God wanted to accomplish through me in the years ahead.

God knew the Israelites couldn't carry out their vital part in His plan of redemption if they didn't observe the principle of rest. He likewise knows you and I can't carry out our roles in his plan for our generation if we ignore that principle today.

---

17. Hebrews 4:11

16

As a people, we are paying a steep price for violating God's principle of rest. Not only is it taking a toll on our minds and bodies, it's damaging our marriages, our families, our careers, and most tragically, our witness to a lost and dying world. (I'll say more about this in Chapter Eight.)

For many years, I didn't understand the value of resting deeply with God and in obedience to His wisdom. But that's not because the Lord didn't try to get through to me. I vividly remember one particular instance from long before I founded Gateway Church. At the time, I was on the pastoral staff of another church.

One day I called a pastor friend of mine to schedule a lunch with him. We both had our calendars out and I said, "What do you have scheduled for next Thursday?"

Him: "Nothing."

Me: "Great!" I replied, "Let's do lunch next Thursday."

Him: "No. Sorry. I can't do Thursday."

Me (confused): "Oh, so you *do* have something on Thursday then?"

Him: "No. I'm doing absolutely nothing on Thursday."

Me (exasperated): "Okay, let's grab lunch then!"

Him: "Robert, you don't understand. I'm looking at my schedule and I have written 'Nothing' on the entire day of Thursday. Next Thursday I am deliberately, intentionally scheduled to do nothing. And nothing is precisely what I plan to do."

Eventually we found a mutually agreeable day to connect. That gave him an opportunity to explain further over lunch. He said, "Robert, as you know, I came very close to dying a few years ago. While I was on my back in the hospital, I had lots of time to talk to God. I remember saying, 'Lord, I'm your servant. I try to serve you. I'm trying my hardest to do what you've called me to do. I don't understand why I'm so sick!' Then the Lord gently but firmly replied to me, 'Son, you've been violating My principles. You violate the Sabbath. You're constantly going and doing. You don't rest one day a week. That's the reason for your health problems. I didn't bring this on you. You brought it on yourself.' Then and there I decided to begin resting one day a week."

Of course, my pastor friend made a full recovery and was stronger and healthier than ever. Over lunch he said, "Now I deliberately schedule time to do nothing one day each week. I've learned that if I don't schedule it, it won't happen."

The Lord tried to help me through my friend that day, but I didn't get the message. All those years ago He was giving me a glimpse of where I would end up if I didn't take hold of the principle my friend was proclaiming to me. It was as if He was lovingly saying, "I have important things for you to do down the road, Robert. Things you can't even imagine right now. But if you don't learn to honor this principle, the day will come when you no longer have a choice but to stop and rest. You can't break my principles. You can only break yourself upon them."

Of course, you already know the punch line to this story. I didn't heed that warning. And eventually, years later, I hit the wall. As I've said, entering a lifestyle of rest is a step of faith. Once I got that revelation and took that step, I got serious about the principle of rest. It may take a while for God to get something through my head, but once He does, I grab hold and don't let go.

> Entering a lifestyle of rest is a step of faith.

Rest: Better Late Than Never

As the founding pastor of a church in hyper-growth mode, I knew I needed to make some significant adjustments in my work life if I was going to truly incorporate the fourth commandment's wisdom into my life. As a church, we had already begun having multiple services each day on both Saturday and Sunday. The weekends were my busiest, most physically, emotionally, and spiritually taxing days of the week. And the weekdays tended to be filled to overflowing with meetings, ministry travel, working breakfasts, working lunches, and sermon preparation.

For the tribes of Israel, Saturday was their only option for a day of rest. God had very explicitly commanded that the seventh day of the week be set aside for rest because He rested from His creative labors after the sixth day. There are some Christian streams and denominations today that contend that Saturday is the only day of rest that is acceptable to God. For example, the Seventh-day Adventist denomination felt so strongly about it, they put it right there in their name! Now, I've met many sweet Seventh-day Adventist folks through the years, but this view can cross the line into legalism.

Please remember, in the New Covenant we're not attempting to keep the letter of the law. That's impossible anyway.[18] We're honoring the eternal principles contained in God's commandments while continuing to stand in Jesus' finished work on the cross for our righteousness and right standing with God. The Pharisees harshly criticized Jesus for healing on the Sabbath. They'd lost sight of the *spirit* of the law and were hung up on being sticklers about the *letter* of the law.

The principle of the Sabbath is to set aside and protect one day out of seven and devote it to rest and fellowship with God. In this New Covenant era, it isn't essential that this special day be Saturday. That's good news for pastors who preach on Saturday, and others whose professions require them to work on Saturday. Another day will do just fine.

---

18. See Romans 7. Paul explains that the law was given to show mankind that we are sinful and in need of a Redeemer.

Decades ahead of me, my pastor friend had discovered a major key to not only surviving but actually thriving. The principle is simply that one day in seven is to be set aside and fiercely protected. It doesn't matter what day of the week that is. I picked Monday as my weekly Sabbath. However, once I embraced that principle and began to institute it, I quickly discovered that the entire world was constantly conspiring to pull me off of that stand. I learned I frequently had to be firm and occasionally downright ruthless in protecting that day against invitations and intrusions. Most of these came from good people with the best of intentions.

I learned to be very clear with our church staff, my friends, and my colleagues around the country. At first, I called my new scheduled-to-do-nothing day "my day off" but I found that term didn't convey the importance and holiness of what that day meant to me and to the God I serve. I would get an invitation to go do something on a Monday and would reply, "I'm sorry, I can't do that. Monday is my day off." To the hearer, it just sounded like I was being selfish and lazy. I eventually learned to say, "I'm sorry. Monday is my Sabbath day. It's holy to the Lord. I'm committed before God to honor that principle in my life. Is there another day we could do that?"

Before long, most of the people in my life came to understand this firm stand, and those invitations became less frequent. Those who loved me the most tended to be the most understanding because they saw the fruit that honoring the Sabbath bore in my life. They saw me growing healthier. Happier. Sharper. Kinder. Everyone loved the healthier, happier, sharper, kinder Robert. If I hadn't insisted on honoring the Sabbath, they probably would have insisted for me!

Nevertheless, I still have to be firm occasionally and do a little teaching in the process. I recall one instance when a staff member—one who had been around long enough to know better—came to me and said, "Hey, I know Monday is your day off, but it would be great if you could attend this [event of some sort]. It's a great cause!"

In order to make a point, I pretended to be offended and said, "Would you encourage me to commit adultery for a good cause? Would you ask me to steal or lie for a good cause? I'm asking because you just asked me to break one of the Ten Commandments. Is breaking commandments okay if it's for a good cause?" My smile broke the momentary awkward tension and let the staff member know I wasn't really angry. But he did get the point—namely that my "day off" is a serious, important, and holy thing to me. I'm hoping that before you've turned the final page of this book, it will be the same for you, too.

God is serious about your rest. And in the aftermath of my underwear and socks episode, we got serious about it as a church. One of the first changes we made was to institute a sabbatical policy for all staff pastors. (More on sabbaticals in Chapter Six.) Furthermore, the church's elders insisted that it begin with me. Immediately. They could all see that I was burned-out and running on fumes. They insisted that I take some time away to rest, refresh, and recharge.

> God is serious about your rest.

I had indeed been running flat out for more than five years since launching the church. So, the church elders voted unanimously to give me six weeks of paid sabbatical leave. That meant I was going to get to unplug for six whole weeks! That seemed like an eternity to me. Sure, I was so utterly weary at every level of my existence that I hardly knew my own name. But I assumed six weeks of leisure was more than enough to recharge my batteries. I was wrong.

As the end of that six-week getaway approached. I began to feel a rising sense of distress. I was doing nothing but hanging out with Debbie, reading, taking walks, and fellowshipping with God, yet I still felt drained. I wasn't feeling anything like the sense of restoration and renewal I'd expected to feel at that point. Alarmed, I added two weeks of unused vacation time to my sabbatical to extend it to eight full weeks. I really did not know what else to do. I had been diligent to rest, relax, and do only things that I found fun and refreshing. I was doing my best to rest, yet I still felt spent.

Then, one morning in the middle of that two-week extension of my sabbatical, I awakened and sensed that everything was different. I realized it while I was reading a book. Suddenly, I felt a wave of relief roll through me. *I'm back!* Out loud, I proclaimed with surprise and delight, "Hey! I'm refreshed!" I felt like the person I was before I started the church five years earlier.

For five years I had been running flat out with only sporadic days of anything resembling rest. I had never been a senior pastor before, much less one leading a church growing at a crazy clip. I didn't know how to handle the work. I didn't know how to arrange my schedule. And most significantly, I didn't know to honor and prioritize the principle of the Sabbath. In fact, in that fifth year, I was no longer taking *any* time away. I took zero Sabbaths for that entire year.

In the moment I realized I felt like myself again, I heard the familiar inward voice of the Lord quietly ask me, "How many days have you been on vacation and at rest?" I counted it up and it was the fifty-third day of my sabbatical. Then I heard the Lord say, "You owed fifty-two days of rest. One year of Sabbaths."

I remember questioning Him in response, "Oh, you mean I owed You fifty-two days?"

"No," He replied, "I didn't say you owed *Me.* Actually, you owed *you* fifty-two days. Robert, the Sabbath is not for My benefit; it's for yours." Right then, I knew never to rob myself of the Sabbath again.

THE FORGOTTEN COMMANDMENT

I felt supernaturally refreshed and renewed after I'd repaid myself that entire year of neglected Sabbath days.

> I felt supernaturally refreshed and renewed.

Is that possible? Could unobserved Sabbaths accumulate against a person? Or a nation? We find the surprising answer in Second Chronicles:

> Then his army burned the Temple of God, tore down the walls of Jerusalem, burned all the palaces, and completely destroyed everything of value. The few who survived were taken as exiles to Babylon, and they became servants to the king and his sons until the kingdom of Persia came to power.
>
> So the message of the LORD spoken through Jeremiah was fulfilled. The land finally enjoyed its Sabbath rest, lying desolate until the seventy years were fulfilled, just as the prophet had said.[19]

We already learned that God had commanded the Israelites to rest one day of every seven. But did you know that He also commanded them to allow the land to rest one year of every seven? He did! Farmland in the land of promise was to be left fallow every seventh year—a Sabbath year for the land. The Lord gave this instruction to Moses on Mount Sinai:

> "When you come into the land which I give you, then the land shall keep a sabbath to the LORD. Six years you shall sow your field, and six years you shall prune your vineyard, and gather its fruit; but in the seventh year there shall be a sabbath of solemn

19. 2 Chronicles 36:19–21 NLT

rest for the land, a sabbath to the LORD. You shall neither sow your field nor prune your vineyard. What grows of its own accord of your harvest you shall not reap, nor gather the grapes of your untended vine, for it is a year of rest for the land"[20]

As with pretty much everything else God instructed the Israelites to do, this is actually a wise and prudent thing to do. Agricultural researchers have proven that land will produce more if farmers let a field rest every few years. Nutrients in the soil become depleted, and resting the land allows it to recuperate. Today, farmers rotate crops and use large amounts of fertilizer in an attempt to achieve the same effect. But in a much less healthy or natural way.

However, as we just read in Second Chronicles, the nation of Israel did not follow this command. They didn't trust God to provide for them in the Sabbath year. That passage suggests that the children of Israel neglected the land's Sabbath, generation after generation for 490 total years. That's right, 490 years! That accumulates to seventy missed years of Sabbath rest for the land.

Eventually the nation of Judah was overrun by the Babylonians and carried off into exile. While the nation was captive in Babylon, the fields of Israel lay fallow and unplanted year after year. Would you like to guess how many years Israel remained in captivity? That's correct. As the writer of Second Chronicles pointed out in the passage above, they were in exile for precisely seventy years. And Second Chronicles 36:21 directly connects those two facts in declaring, *"The land finally enjoyed its Sabbath rest, lying desolate until the seventy years were fulfilled."* (emphasis added). The bill ultimately came due and Judah was not restored to their land until it was paid in full.

---

20. Leviticus 25:2–5

The people of Israel might have assumed that God wasn't serious about His command of letting the land rest every seventh year. After all, they seemed to get away with it, decade after decade, century after century. In a similar way, I thought I could ignore God's command to rest one day out of seven. I thought I was getting away with it. But as you now know, that bill eventually came due, as well. I repaid myself my fifty-two days of neglected Sabbaths all in one stretch.

Notice that God said, "the land finally *enjoyed* its Sabbath rest." If God is concerned about the land enjoying rest, how much more is He concerned about you enjoying yours? Is it possible that you owe yourself some rest days? Our good, gracious, loving Father God designated the Sabbath for our good. He wants us to *enjoy* it. Rest is part of God's good plan for you. A Master Designer created you that way.

> God said, "the land finally *enjoyed* its Sabbath rest."

Did the description at the beginning of this book about living life without margin sound familiar? Well, Jesus' invitation still stands:

"Come to Me, all you who labor and are heavy laden, and I will give you rest. Take My yoke upon you and learn from Me, for I am gentle and lowly in heart, and you will find rest for your souls. For My yoke is easy and My burden is light"[21]

Let's take another step on this journey into rest by examining one of the biggest obstacles you'll face along the way: your own good intentions.

---

21. Matthew 11:28–30

CHAPTER TWO

WHO HAS TIME TO REST?

People expect us to be busy, overworked. It's become a status symbol in our society—if we are busy, we're important; if we're not busy, we're almost embarrassed to admit it.
                              —Stephen Covey, *First Things First*

The report submitted to the government of Japan simply called him "Mr. A." to protect his identity. Let's call him Mr. Asako. He had worked for several years at a major Japanese snack food processing company, often putting in as many as 110 hours each week. Just to put that into perspective, that's more than two and a half forty-hour work weeks jammed into one. To log 110 hours in a week requires working nearly sixteen hours per day for seven days. He did that week after week. Year after year.

They found Mr. Asako dead at his work station, the victim of a heart attack.

He was thirty-four.[1]

In Japan they call it *karōshi*. The Chinese have their own word for it: *guolaosi*. And in South Korea they call it *gwarosa*. All three terms

---

1. "Case Study: Karoshi: Death from Overwork," Ilo.org, 2013, http://www
.ilo.org/safework/info/publications/WCMS_211571/lang--en/index.htm.

were coined fairly recently to describe something so new that their languages didn't have a word for it. These words describe the act of literally working yourself to death. All three of these cultures discovered they needed a word to describe an increasingly common phenomenon: people dropping dead at their jobs as a result of working insane hours, under intense pressure, with little to no rest. It has become so common, in fact, that international human rights organizations are calling on the governments of those nations to do something about it.[2]

Why is this phenomenon emerging in Asia? Well, for one thing that part of the world doesn't have a foundational Christian heritage like the one upon which Western civilization was built. And Christianity has Jewish roots. In fact, numerous secular experts on ancient history credit the Jewish people with the invention of the seven-day week containing a day of rest. It's a distinctly Judeo-Christian concept.[3] Without that cultural foundation, many employers in Asia have no qualms about demanding that employees work long hours, seven days a week. One article on the *karōshi* phenomenon said, "It is not uncommon for many Japanese employees to work late hours until 2:00 or 3:00 a.m., then be expected to be in the office again at 9:00 a.m."[4]

I don't have to tell you that our culture's biblical foundation has been under attack for decades now. As a people, it seems we've been trying to sever our ties to our Christian roots as fast as we can. Even

---

2. "Case Study: Karoshi."

3. See quote from Rutgers University professor Dr. Eviatar Zerubavel: "A continuous seven-day cycle that runs throughout history paying no attention whatsoever to the moon and its phases is a distinctively Jewish invention." *The Seven Day Circle: The History and Meaning of the Week* (Chicago: University of Chicago Press, 1985), 11.

4. Edwin Lane, "The Young Japanese Working Themselves to Death," BBC News, 2017, https://www.bbc.com/news/business-39981997.

so, our culture contains enough remnants of our Christian values and ethics to provide at least some residual respect for the Sabbath in our culture. Forty years ago, most stores in America were closed on Sunday. No longer, with the exception of a few Christian-owned companies such as Chick-fil-A and Hobby Lobby. These Asian cultures have no corresponding historical tradition of resting one day each week. As a result, that part of the world is experiencing an alarming epidemic of *karōshi* deaths. Right alongside this tragic trend, the Japanese have had to come up with another new word. *Karōjisatsu* is the word they've given to being driven to commit suicide because of the depression and weariness from being overworked. This, too, is a rising phenomenon in Asia.[5] As we've already clearly seen, a failure to rest regularly devastates not only the body but the mind and emotions as well. For increasing numbers of overworked people in these cultures, suicide seems to be the only pathway to rest.

Please understand, I'm not singling out these cultures for criticism. We Americans haven't yet gotten around to creating an English word for working oneself to death, but we'll likely need one soon. I'd suggest "Sabbath Deficiency Syndrome," but that's probably too wordy to catch on. For Americans, it's not necessarily about working sixteen hours a day, seven days a week at one job. It's more about allowing ourselves to be pulled in a dozen different directions all the time, every day. We have demanding full-time jobs plus countless other things vying for attention. We're chronically, unendingly, terminally busy.

Busyness is often more than a mere habit. For many it's actually an

---

5. Michiaki Okuyama, "The Suicide Problem in Contemporary Japanese Society: Its Economic and Social Backdrop and Religious Reactions," Researchmap. jp, 2009, https://researchmap.jp/mu9mbahfh-2096/?

addiction. One that's as powerful and controlling as any addiction to alcohol or drugs. The difference is that our culture still frowns upon being addicted to chemicals but actually encourages and rewards our addiction

> There's no negative social stigma associated with being addicted to "busy."

to being hurried, harried, and overscheduled. There's no negative social stigma associated with being addicted to "busy." Most drug addicts and alcoholics are in denial. But busy addicts own it proudly. In fact, a 2019 survey revealed that nearly half (48 percent) of Americans actually consider themselves workaholics. More than half of the people who took the survey said they were feeling stressed-out from work as they were taking the survey![6] These people were likely not confessing something they were ashamed of. I suspect most were actually bragging. As the quote by Stephen Covey at the top of this chapter notes, being stretched to the breaking point has somehow become a status symbol in our culture. Please note that Covey wrote those words back in 1995. Our idolization of "busy" has only worsened over the last twenty-five years.

Referring to the toll of living with our addiction and idolization of "busy," Canadian author and pastor Mark Buchanan writes:

And something dies in us. Too much work, the British used to say, makes Jack a dull boy. But it's worse than that. It numbs Jack, parches Jack, hardens Jack. It kills his heart. When we get too busy, everything becomes either a trudge or a scramble, the doldrums or sheer mayhem. We get bored with the

---

6. Tyler Schmall, "Almost Half of Americans Consider Themselves 'Workaholics,'" NYPost.com, 2019, https://nypost.com/2019/02/01/almost-half-of-americans-consider-themselves-workaholics/.

familiar, threatened by the unfamiliar. Our capacity for both steadfastness and adventure shrivels.[7]

Too Much of a Good Thing

I can hear the self-appointed internet critics now: "That Robert Morris fellow doesn't believe in the good old American work ethic. He's preaching against hard work!"

Of course, that's not true at all. There's nothing biblical or virtuous about laziness. The Bible's premier wisdom book, Proverbs, is filled with warnings against being idle or lazy. (Just do a word search in Proverbs on the term "sluggard.") What's more, we often forget that God's commandment about the Sabbath contains a flip side. God said, "Six days you shall labor and do all your work."[8] That's right, God's direct command to rest one day out of seven is built upon the assumption that you're going to put in six good, vigorous days of work in your vocation and around your home.

Precisely what that six days of work looks like for most of us in our modern, urbanized world is very different than it was for the farmers and shepherds of Israel. They tended to spend all six days, from sunup to sundown, doing basically the same thing. That is, tending to the farm or the flocks and the homestead. That has been true throughout most of history. Most of our great-grandparents lived pretty much the same way in this country.

Today, most of us work five-day-a-week jobs. For many those jobs

7. Mark Buchanan, *The Rest of God: Restoring Your Soul by Restoring Sabbath*, Kindle ed. (repr., Nashville, Tennessee: Thomas Nelson, 2006), 47.
8. Exodus 20:9

involve a lengthy commute to and from the workplace. It's not unusual for someone to leave the house before sunrise and not return until the sun has set. We then attempt to attend to everything related to house, yard, and family on the nights and weekends. Around all of this we cram in events, obligations, clubs, second jobs, and, for parents with kids at home, their endless school projects and extracurricular activities.

The rise of smartphones has enabled us to pour online activity—particularly social media consumption—into every crack and crevice of our already overfilled schedules. This wouldn't be quite as problematic if social media tended to have a calming, encouraging, or nourishing effect on our souls. You know that's not the case. The vast majority of our social media feeds and news feeds represent an unending stream of bad news, atrocity, and catastrophe. Our fallen world is filled with things to be either grieved or outraged about—and now we carry in our hands a device that brings all of it to our attention, all the time. Even when someone posts something good or spiritual or encouraging, we'll often see a comment beneath it that makes us angry. Comment threads on the internet are some of the darkest, most negative, most strife-ridden places in existence.

Other social media platforms are more about making you feel inadequate, unlovely, uncool, or boring. They create the illusion that everyone you know is living a better life than you. They're eating at better restaurants, taking better vacations, enjoying cuter pets, and just generally being happy all the time. It's not just hard work that's exhausting us physically, emotionally, and mentally.

For most of us, our phones are within reach twenty-four hours a day, seven days a week. They've become our default focal point in every quiet moment or halt in activity. Standing in line at the store? Pull out the phone. Stopped at a red light? Look at the phone. A momentary lull in the conversation with the spouse or a friend? Check the phone. We've essentially hooked ourselves up to a constant IV drip of worry, outrage, fear, and negativity inserted directly into our already weary souls.

No, there is nothing wrong with hard work. It's important. God's wisdom principles encourage diligence and excellence. But consistent hard work is only sustainable if we honor another of God's immutable, unchangeable principles. The principle of rest.

> God's wisdom principles encourage diligence and excellence.

Work is not the enemy. The temptation to not rest is the enemy. So, why don't we?

Noble Motives, Out of Balance

Often, we refuse to rest out of a noble sense of responsibility that drives us to work as much as we possibly can. Many men derive a significant portion of their sense of identity from being a "good provider" for their families. Women often feel enormous pressure to be all things to all people, frequently pursuing a career or at least providing a second income *and* fulfilling the more traditional role of running the household at the same time. Of course, single mothers and fathers have no choice but to do everything and be everything.

We don't want anyone to accuse us of not providing for our families or holding up our end. Those of us who have been in church all our lives have Paul's strong words to Timothy ringing in the ears of our spirits: "But if anyone does not provide for his own, and especially for those of his household, he has denied the faith and is worse than an unbeliever."[9]

Worse than an unbeliever! No Christian would ever want to be guilty of a sin that brought that kind of indictment. We say to

---

9. 1 Timothy 5:8

ourselves, "Message received. I must provide for my family at all costs." This mandate actually provides a seemingly righteous rationalization for ignoring God's command to rest one day out of seven. However, in order for us to understand the true meaning of Paul's words, we have to view them in the light of God's commandments. You wouldn't try to rationalize stealing in the name of "providing for my family." You would recognize that God wouldn't have you violate one command in order to obey another, as we've already seen. Choosing to obey the command to rest is a step of faith, comparable to giving God the first 10 percent of your income. It requires trust in God to supernaturally help you fulfill all your responsibilities in the six remaining days each week. And I'm here to tell you, He will!

You're not failing as a provider when, in faith and trust in God, you set aside one day each week to recharge and renew. Nor are you less significant or valuable when you're scheduled to do nothing—contrary to what the spirit of our times would have you believe. In fact, the opposite is true. Learning to rest actually helps you fulfill your responsibilities. By giving both your body and your soul rest, you become more effective and efficient at everything you do the other six days each week. This is what Stephen Covey would call "sharpening the saw." This concept is an echo of a wise quote attributed to Abraham Lincoln:

> By giving both your body and your soul rest, you become more effective and efficient at everything you do the other six days each week.

Give me six hours to chop down a tree and I will spend the first four sharpening the axe.[10]

---

10. Daniel Coenn, *Abraham Lincoln: His Words*, Kindle ed. (BookRix, 2014).

TAKE THE DAY OFF

The point is, you'll be more effective and productive in six days with rest, than you will be in seven days without it. Again, God's commands are always for our benefit. God is not throwing additional hurdles and obstacles in front of you. He's trying to help you. The Sabbath is not the only way God sets us apart as His unique people. The principle of the Sabbath is a gift! It is a weekly celebration, a party even. The rest of the ancient world commemorated their idols with annual religious feasts, but the God of Israel gave His people a weekly feast—a day to gather with family, to relax, to rest, and to be refreshed. A day to celebrate that we are the people of God and that He is good.

Yes, real, weekly rest is difficult. Everything in our modern world seems to work against it. But don't make the mistake of thinking it was easy in ancient times. Imagine life before supermarkets, clothes washers, cars, or indoor plumbing. Everything required long, tedious manual labor. Even if you practiced a trade like metalworking or carpentry, you still likely owned livestock and tended crops. The approach of winter required extra preparation and storing away of food and supplies. The fact is, honoring the principle of the Sabbath required faith and trust in God back then. It still does today.

Redeeming Rest

Look again at that entire key passage in Hebrews. The Amplified translation is illuminating:

And to whom did He swear that they should not enter His rest, but to those who *disobeyed* [who had not listened to His word and who refused to be compliant or be persuaded]? So we see that they were not able to enter [into His rest], because of their unwillingness to adhere to and trust in and rely on God [*unbelief had shut them out*].

Therefore, while the promise of entering His rest still holds and is offered [today], let us be afraid [to distrust it], lest any of you should think he has come too late and has come short of [reaching] it. For indeed we have had the glad tidings [Gospel of God] proclaimed to us just as truly as they [the Israelites of old did when the good news of deliverance from bondage came to them]; but the message they heard did not benefit them, because it was not mixed with faith (with the leaning of the entire personality on God in absolute trust and confidence in His power, wisdom, and goodness) by those who heard it; neither were they united in faith with the ones [Joshua and Caleb] who heard (did believe)"[11]

What, according to this passage in Hebrews, prevents us from entering God's rest? Disobedience and unbelief. The Israelites' unbelief—or put another way, their lack of faith and trust in God—produced a hard-hearted refusal to lean their "entire personality on God in absolute trust and confidence in His power, wisdom, and goodness." The only alternative to trusting in God is trusting in self. Placing confidence in our own efforts and ability. This prevented the Israelites from entering the rest the Lord very much wanted to give them.

Please keep in mind, these people had been slaves in Egypt for four hundred years. In the tense, drama-filled months leading up to their deliverance from Egypt as Moses confronted Pharaoh, their Egyptian taskmasters responded by increasing their burdens and putting impossible demands on them. Then, by God's miraculous, mighty hand,

---

11. 3:18–4:2 AMPC

> The Lord demonstrated His great love for them.

they left Egypt and began a long, arduous journey through the Red Sea and into the rugged desert of the Sinai Peninsula. If any people ever needed some rest, they did. The Lord demonstrated His great love for them, miraculously provided for them, and revealed His presence in numerous ways. Yet that generation of Israelites never trusted God enough to believe that He was leading them to a good place. The promised land would be a place of rest for them. But disobedience and distrust disqualified them from entering in.

Centuries later, Isaiah delivered a prophetic word to Judah that predicted impending judgment. In it, we find these haunting words:

For thus the Lord GOD, the Holy One of Israel, has said, "In repentance and rest you will be saved, In quietness and trust is your strength." But you were not willing...[12]

Even in the days prior to them being carried off into captivity in Babylon, God was still pleading with His people to enter into the rest He wanted to give them. He reminds them that they will gain strength if they'll just trust Him and get quiet before Him. But Isaiah follows God's tender plea with an indictment: "But you were not willing." How tragic!

Before we judge Judah too harshly, we need to recognize that we often do the same thing. God says, "rest." Yet so often we are unwilling. Rest is a gift from God but it requires faith to receive it.

---

12. Isaiah 30:15–16 NASB

Redeeming Work

We've already observed that God's commandment about resting one day out of seven also contained the assumption that the remaining six days are for work. So, we shouldn't be surprised to discover that God cares about our work life as much as we do.

Our waking moments are largely filled with talking about work, thinking about work, planning for work, looking forward to work, or dreading work. We feel guilty if we don't do enough of it, or we feel resentful when we work too much. Our lives revolve around work, but often it's not the actual work that exhausts us. It's the worry, fretting, stress, and anxiety about it that wears us out. That was certainly the case with me in the years before I understood and embraced the principle of the Sabbath and set clear, firm boundaries around my "day off." Prior to that awakening, any time I took a day off, I sat around obsessing about all the things that weren't getting done and feeling guilty the entire day. My mental work was stealing my spiritual rest.

The truth is, work—that is, meaningful, productive things to do that bear fruit—is a divine gift of God. Understanding the gift of work helps us better appreciate the gift of rest. Some people mistakenly assume that work came into being as a part of the curse that befell mankind after sin entered the world. Work is not a part of the curse! Work existed before Adam fell. Please note these words from the second chapter of Genesis:

Then the LORD God took the man and put him in the Garden of Eden to tend it and keep it.[13]

---

13. Genesis 2:15

TAKE THE DAY OFF

Do you see it? God gave man a job before sin caused the Fall. Why did He create work? Because God loves us! He wants us to do something that rewards and fulfills us. The Lord doesn't want us to sit around being bored, without anything to accomplish. He gave each of us the gift of work. We can engage our minds and our hands in work, and after investing some time and energy, we can step back from it and feel genu-inely fulfilled. We feel rewarded because we have accomplished something.

> We feel rewarded because we have accomplished something.

Yes, God gave us work because He loves us. However, the curse made work much, much harder. Because Adam ate from the tree of knowledge of good and evil, God informed him of the terrible consequences of his act:

"Cursed is the ground for your sake; In toil you shall eat of it all the days of your life. Both thorns and thistles it shall bring forth for you, and you shall eat the herb of the field. In the sweat of your face you shall eat bread..."[14]

Toil and sweat. That's how the curse changed the nature of work. The curse turned work into hard labor. Fruitfulness and productivity would now only come with more difficulty and effort. Have you ever had one of those days at work? I'm talking about a day that seems as if all your energy goes into thorns and thistles—prickly people, sticky situations. Then, just when it seems you have cleared one area, more weeds pop up somewhere else.

14. Genesis 3:17–19

That is the reality of this fallen world, but I have wonderful news. Jesus Christ redeemed us from the curse.[15] For the born-again believer, Jesus has provided a way to view work that rises above the sweat and toil of this world. Just as you've been redeemed by the work of Jesus on the cross, your work has been redeemed as well! You can now view your work as Adam did before the Fall. Whatever it is you do, can and should be done to the glory of God.[16] Whatever you do, no matter how mundane it seems, is actually a form of worship that brings glory and pleasure to God. In fact, the Hebrew word sometimes translated as "work" in the Old Testament, *avodah*, also carries the meaning "to worship." In fact, *avodah* is variously translated "work," "worship," or "service" in your Bible, depending upon the context. For example, in Genesis 2:5, before God created man, the Word of God notes: "...and there was no one to work (*avodah*) the ground."[17] Ten verses later, we read, "The LORD God took the man and put him in the Garden of Eden to work (*avodah*) it and take care of it."[18] Yet in Exodus 8:1 God says, "Let my people go, so that they may worship (*avodah*) me."[19]

There's a message for us in this. It tells us that our work can be a form of worship where we simultaneously honor the Lord through our excellence and diligence, serve our families by providing for them, and serve our communities by adding value. For the believer,

---

15. See Galatians 3:13

16. See Colossians 3:23-24 NLT: "Work willingly at whatever you do, as though you were working for the Lord rather than for people. Remember that the Lord will give you an inheritance as your reward, and that the Master you are serving is Christ."

17. NIV

18. Genesis 2:15 NIV

19. NIV

work done as worship advances God's kingdom. Yes, as a citizen of the kingdom of God, your work has kingdom implications.

When work consistently feels like dreaded drudgery, that's a warning indicator about one of two things: either you're not honoring the principle of rest in your life and are therefore burned-out, or you need a paradigm shift about the sacred nature of work. You need to start seeing it as something that blesses God and carries kingdom implications. In other words, you need to redeem your work life.

Begin to make a practice of thanking God for your work. Gratitude opens the door to His kingdom. Even if you think you hate everything about your current job, you can find *something* to thank God for about your work. Anything! Maybe you like the color of the tile in the office restroom. Then begin by thanking Him for that. By shifting into an attitude of gratitude and positivity, you'll set yourself on a path moving toward viewing your work as *avodah*, that is, an act of worship with kingdom implications. Pastor Mark Buchanan had this shift in mind when he wrote:

What if your work became worship? What if the work of your hands—repairing lawn mowers, scouring pots, paving streets, mending bones, balancing ledgers—was Eucharistic, a sacrament of God's presence that you gave and received? What if Jesus himself was your boss, the One who watched over you and whom you honored with your efforts? Here's a radical idea: next time you're tempted to complain about your work, praise God for it instead. Next time you open your mouth to gossip about people you work with or smear those you work for, stop yourself and turn in the other direction:

> Begin to make a practice of thanking God for your work.

pray for them, thank God for them, find the good in them. Next time you want to quit, pour that into worship.[20]

The enemy of your soul uses the thorns and thistles of this world to discourage you from transforming your work into worship. God's mortal enemy doesn't want you discovering and cultivating your God-given vocation. Dig deep anyway. Press through.

By the way, do you know where we get the word "vocation?" It comes from the Latin word *vocare*, which means to call or to name. Your vocation is God calling you out for something unique to you. That voice deep inside of you is God telling you what He created you to do. He wants you to heed His call.

What I'm talking about requires erasing the man-made dividing line between work and ministry. What jobs and careers come to your mind when I use the phrase, "the Lord's work"? If I were to say that someone is involved in "the work of the Lord," what would you assume that person does? I suspect you would instantly think of a pastor, a missionary, or someone in full-time ministry. At the same time, if you're like most people, you think of accountants, salespeople, butchers, bakers, and candlestick makers as having secular or worldly jobs. You know, regular, nonspiritual jobs.

This line of separation is artificial and unbiblical. That fact is, if you belong to God, whatever you do is "the work of the Lord" for you. Yet for some reason, we don't think that when God creates and calls a firefighter, that he or she is "in ministry" or having an impact for the kingdom of God. That's false! Believers who think like this tend to view only the volunteer work they do for or through their

---

20. Mark Buchanan, *The Rest of God: Restoring Your Soul by Restoring Sabbath*, Kindle ed. (repr., Nashville, Tennessee: Thomas Nelson, 2006), 27.

church as real ministry. This mistake turns the thing they do for the majority of their waking hours each week into a secular thing—something too low or mundane for God to be involved in.

Please stop thinking that way. Whatever you do for a living as a child of God is *not* secular. It's sacred.

Redeeming Time

Some time ago, I received an email from a person I have known for several years. He invited me to lunch to reconnect. A quick check of my calendar revealed that I would not be able to meet him for quite a while. For weeks, every single day with the exception of my Sabbaths were quite full. So, I emailed back a sympathetic but straightforwardly honest reply: "I'm really sorry; I value our relationship, but I can't get together right now. My schedule is full."

Immediately, he emailed back, hoping for a reversal of my decision on appeal: "Can't you make time for me?"

I understood the question. I'm sure I had asked others to make time for me in the past. But with my hard-won understanding of how important time is to God, and of the need to protect my God-given priorities, I replied, "I cannot, my friend. Only God can make time. In fact, He's already made all the time there's ever going to be. I wish I could, but I cannot make even one extra hour."

Doesn't it sometimes seem like that is all in the world we need? Just one extra hour? I half jokingly asked God for that once—just one extra hour per day, every day. At the root of my desperate prayer was an assumption. I had somehow convinced myself that with only one additional hour per day, I could finally stop feeling behind on everything and under pressure all the time. Of course, that's a delusion. It's a fallacy very similar to a common one about money. Everyone under financial pressure truly believes that with just a little more income, everything would be great.

> More time is not the answer. Better stewardship of time is the answer.

But it wouldn't. More money never fixes the internal and systemic stewardship issues that create financial pressure in the first place. The same is true with time. More time is not the answer. Better stewardship of time is the answer.

My colleague and I did connect at a later time. He didn't hold a grudge against me and, in fact, he told me he respected the firm stand I took. He said it had inspired him to set firmer boundaries concerning all the requests he tended to get for his time.

No, we cannot "make time." Nor can we "save" time. Does that surprise you? We constantly hear talk about time-saving devices and saving time through special techniques and shortcuts. We essentially talk about time much in the same way we do about money. Yet we really *can* save money. But we can only spend, manage, and invest time. We can never save it. You can't bank two of today's hours so you can withdraw and use them a few weeks from now when you desperately need a twenty-six-hour day. If time is like money, then we are all on a fixed income. There is no wealth inequality or disparity with time. You, I, Bill Gates, Warren Buffett, and the homeless guy living beneath the overpass are all given the exact same allotment of 1,440 minutes every day.

The only thing that differentiates us is how we choose to use those minutes. Time is the great equalizer.

Making choices about time is what's known as a *zero-sum game*. One hour applied to Thing A means that hour can never be applied to Thing B. Saying yes to an invitation to meet with someone is unavoidably a choice not to spend that time studying, being with my family, or imparting to our staff. I simply cannot make more time. Nor can you. The only power we have is the power to choose.

I have come to this understanding slowly and with much difficulty. I spent a good chunk of my life determined to find ways to save time. I still catch myself doing it. At the bank drive-through lanes, I study the lane options like some kind of bank traffic scientist. I count the cars in each lane taking care not to be fooled by cars that are extra short or extra long. I look to see who is retrieving items from the little pneumatic tubes and who is just putting things in. I feel sure I can deduce which lane is going to get me through and on my way the quickest.

I have never been right. Not once!

Invariably, I choose the line with the person who seems to be trying to negotiate a home loan with the teller. I sit there fuming and trapped as the lanes on either side of me flow forward like a mighty river. I watch with frustrated envy as those drivers speed away, their banking business complete, heading on to accomplish other tasks. I go through similar exercises in heavy freeway traffic and at the grocery store. My lane-picking expertise fares no better in those settings. It's always the *other* lanes moving faster.

I have discovered that the more I try to save time, the more I actually squander it. Here is an all-too-common scenario: You pick your child up from school and, while she is telling you about her day, you think, "Maybe I can organize my thoughts for tomorrow's meeting while she's talking?" As you drift off in your mind, you are actually wasting time. In fact, you're squandering a precious and irreplaceable moment. That little girl is never going to be in third grade again. She'll never be eight years old, three months, and four days again. Tomorrow she'll be eight years old, three months, and five days. Your opportunity to be present and engaged in that moment will never come again.

How much precious time have we wasted in futile efforts to save it? You and I cannot save time. We can only spend it.

I vividly recall an instance when I was a guest minister at another church. We were in the worship portion of the service and everyone around me was entering into a spirit of praise and worship to God. Based on the expressions on the faces around me, it was clear that people were experiencing the presence of God. I, on the other hand, was hundreds of miles away in my mind. I was trying to solve a problem I was having back home. I was trying to decide what I was going to say to this person and how I was going to handle that person. Suddenly, my mental gymnastics were interrupted by the clear, firm voice of God.

"What are you doing?"

"Well, Lord," I responded. "I'm trying to work out this problem."

"Oh. Well, everyone else here is worshipping Me."

I got His point. So, I shifted my focus to His goodness and faithfulness to me. And soon I too found myself experiencing the refreshing breeze of His presence. In that moment, the Lord gave me a revelation. I heard Him say, "For the next hour, your sole purpose on earth is to minister to these people. They need your full attention. They need everything you have. I will take care of your problem. I've got it. Meanwhile, I need you to choose to spend this hour wholeheartedly on this group of people."

I've never forgotten the lesson of that day. God brought me back to the present moment and reminded me that this moment, this *now*, is all we have. And it's all we need.

What are you going to do with your time? And most importantly,

> I will take care of your problem. I've got it.

are you going to embrace the principle of the Sabbath and rest? I know that even as you read that question, there are voices in your head telling you you can't do it. That you can't afford to "lose" a day out of your week every week. That it won't work for you.

Those voices have a counterpart in the Bible. Let me explain.

As we've already seen, we find God giving Moses and the Israelites the Ten Commandments, including the fourth commandment concerning the Sabbath, in Exodus Chapter 20. But did you know God repeated his command to observe the Sabbath? We find it in the fifth chapter of Deuteronomy. The first time God introduced the Sabbath commandment, He explained it in terms of his six days of creation. He said, "For in six days the Lord made the heavens and the earth, the sea, and all that is in them, and rested the seventh day." But in Deuteronomy, the Lord explains the meaning of the Sabbath in completely different terms:

> "Observe the Sabbath day, to keep it holy, as the LORD your God commanded you. Six days you shall labor and do all your work, but the seventh day is the Sabbath of the LORD your God… *And remember that you were a slave in the land of Egypt*, and the LORD your God brought you out from there by a mighty hand and by an outstretched arm; therefore the LORD your God commanded you to keep the Sabbath day."[21] (emphasis added)

Do you see it? Instead of pointing back to God's creation day labors to explain the Sabbath, God instead points them back to their recent deliverance from slavery. This is an interesting distinction.

God's people had been slaves for centuries. Slaves cannot rest. They cannot choose to take a day off from work. A taskmaster stands over a slave with a whip and demands that the slave continues

---

21. Deuteronomy 5:12–15

to work without resting. The Sabbath reminds us that God, in His mercy, drowned the Egyptian taskmasters in the sea.

In a sense, many of us have pulled those taskmasters out of the depths of the sea and given them CPR! Anytime you try to rest, they stand over you with a whip. They are those voices in your head I mentioned a moment ago. *What do you think you're doing? Have you forgotten all the things that you need to be doing right now? Apparently, you have, so I'll list them for you...* This is the voice of your taskmaster. But you are no longer a slave. You have been redeemed.

As I stated at the beginning of this chapter, embracing the Sabbath requires faith. God invites us to experience His rest, but to enter it requires trust in his power and faithfulness. Observing the Sabbath is the primary way we put God first with our time.

> God invites us to experience His rest, but to enter it requires trust in his power and faithfulness.

In his time management book, *First Things First*, which I quoted at the top of this chapter, Stephen Covey relates a powerful illustration of this principle.[22] I shared this story in my book *Beyond Blessed*, but it bears repeating here.

Covey described a group of ambitious MBA students assembled for a seminar on time management. At one point in his presentation, the expert said, "Okay, time for a quiz," and produced a big, widemouthed glass jar, setting it on a table in front of him. Then he brought out a bucket filled with fist-sized rocks. One by one he carefully placed the rocks into the jar until it was filled to the top and no more rocks would fit inside. Then he asked the class, "Is

---

22. Stephen R. Covey, A. Roger Merrill and Rebecca R. Merrill, *First Things First* (New York: Free Press, 1994), 88.

this jar full?" Every head in the class nodded. In response he said, "Really?" He then reached under the table and pulled out a bucket of pea-sized gravel. Then he dumped some gravel into the jar and shook it, causing pieces of gravel to work themselves down into the spaces between the larger rocks until it could contain no more.

Then he smiled and asked the group once more, "Now is the jar full?" By this time the class was wary. "Probably not," one of them answered. "Good!" he replied. And he reached under the table and brought out a bucket of sand and proceeded to dump it in. The sand easily settled into all the spaces left between the rocks and the gravel. Once more he asked the question: "Is this jar full?" No one ventured an opinion. Smiling, the teacher took a pitcher of water and poured it in until the jar was filled to the brim. Then he looked up at the group and asked, "Can anyone tell me what the point of this illustration is?"

One attendee raised his hand and ventured, "The point is, no matter how full you think your schedule is, you can always fit some more things into it!"

"No," the speaker replied, "that's not the point. The truth this illustration teaches us is: if you don't put the big rocks in first, you'll never get them in at all." From a time management standpoint, the lesson is that we have to *schedule* and *protect* the most important things we want to accomplish. Otherwise, you'll never fit them in. We have to put the big rocks in first.

It's true! Now allow me to put that a different way. The Sabbath is the biggest of the big rocks where your time is concerned. You may not feel you can afford to honor it. But I'm here to tell you, you cannot afford not to.

We're about to discover that if you don't put in the big rock of rest, your schedule may always be full, but four key parts of who you are will be constantly running on empty.

CHAPTER THREE

THE FOUR TANKS

You are a spirit, you have a soul, and you live in a body.
—Traditional Christian Truism

Ministry has taken me far outside my home state of Texas many times over the years, yet I never stop being surprised by how much more expensive gasoline is in other places. I know lower state taxes on gasoline is one reason it costs so much less to fill up a car in Texas than in many other states. But another big factor is that Texas is where so much of our oil is found, extracted, and refined into gasoline. In other words, gas is cheap here because we make the stuff.

Driving across Texas, you will encounter abundant evidence of just how significant the oil industry is throughout our big state. How big is Texas? For some perspective, the drive from Texarkana to El Paso is 812 miles. That's a twelve-to-thirteen-hour drive providing you never stop to go to the restroom. Along that drive you'll see countless oil wells, refineries, and storage tanks consistently reminding you that you're in oil country. You'll also share the highways with a remarkable number of gasoline tanker trucks, carrying fuel to gas stations all over the central United States. In flat West Texas, you might be driving down the highway, traveling at a leisurely pace, lulled into a bit of a hypnotic trance by a hundred-mile stretch of road without a single curve or bend, when suddenly a huge tanker truck roars by in the passing lane and shakes your entire car. Within seconds, you are more awake than you have been all day. I have had that experience on more than one occasion.

One day, the Lord used one of those tanker trucks as a personal illustration to burn an unforgettable message about my calling as a pastor and teacher into my heart. He said, "Robert, you are a fuel truck. That is your job." Immediately, I envisioned one of those familiar 18-wheelers. The Lord continued: "Your job involves going from station to station to fill up their tanks with the fuel from your truck." I knew immediately what He meant. I have to fill up my family. I have to fill up the elders of our church, the staff, the lay-leadership, and, of course, the membership. It occurred to me that I even supply pastors from other churches because Gateway has grown to be a place to which many churches around the country look for advice and encouragement.

It made sense to me. My job is to refuel other people. But the moment I made the connection of that analogy, I had another realization. The gasoline tanker truck called "Robert Morris" was nearly empty most of the time! I knew I was ministering to everyone with a tank that was nearly dry. And in that moment, God called me out on it.

I've already revealed in detail how I approached those first years after founding Gateway Church. What I haven't revealed is the role misplaced guilt played in my inability to truly take a day of rest.

Fairly early on, I began to try to take one day off per week. "Try" is the key word in that previous sentence. Because we have services on Saturdays and Sundays, Monday made the most sense with my schedule, but most of the rest of the church staff was in the office on Monday. So were all my friends who didn't work at the church.

They were all working away on Monday as well. Thus, I would start to feel guilty for just sitting at home doing nothing, even though I'd just put in a full, utterly draining weekend of work.

Each Monday, everyone I knew was working, so I started feeling like I ought to be doing something, too. A combination of religious obligation and manly pride worked together to convince me that I was doing something wrong by not doing something productive.

It started small. I'd just take a quick peek at email a time or two during the day. "I just need to make sure nothing truly important needs my immediate attention," I rationalized. However, I soon discovered that it really bugged me not to answer an email question or request. So, I started replying to a few email messages. Then more of them. Then most of them. Of course, the fact that I was now responding to email on my day off only encouraged everyone in my life to feel free to email or text me on that day. Before long, I was booking work-related lunches and breakfasts, then getting cleaned up and heading to the office for an occasional important meeting. It escalated relentlessly.

> "I just need to make sure nothing truly important needs my immediate attention," I rationalized.

In the absence of clear boundaries and strong convictions about the principle of the Sabbath, on top of the inappropriate guilt I felt about doing nothing, it was remarkably easy for me to allow my Mondays to turn into just a different kind of workday. Even when I didn't actually do much, that guilty mind-set stole my peace. I had no faith for true rest because I wasn't convinced it was appropriate.

In hindsight, I can clearly see how I was killing myself with work. That's the state I was in when the Lord likened me to a fuel truck with no fuel to share with others.

I remember responding to Him, "God, I know that I'm often ministering to others on only a quarter of a tank. And I can frequently feel myself dipping from a quarter of a tank to near-empty. Somehow, through spending time with You, I'm able to get back up to a quarter of a tank again. And then the draining starts all over again. Lord, you know that I get to where I can't think. I don't have the physical strength to keep up the pace. And even when I manage to show up, I don't have the emotional or mental reserves to properly help anyone."

After accurately diagnosing the situation that the Lord had lovingly brought to my attention, I then offered up what I thought God's ideal looked like. I said, "God, I know you want me to always be ministering to others from a tank that is somewhere between three-quarters and full." Of course, I had no idea how to make that happen, but I was confident that that was the goal.

Then I heard the Lord's reply. He said, "Wrong."

"Excuse me, Lord?"

"I don't want you ministering from a tank that's merely *almost* full. I want you ministering from an *overflowing* tank. A cup that's running over. That's what I want for you, son."

The heavenly Father's words put me in remembrance of the 23rd psalm:

You prepare a table before me in the presence of my enemies;
You anoint my head with oil; My cup runs over.[1]

God dramatically shifted my paradigm. He didn't want me struggling to somehow stay full in the midst of constant demands

---

1. Psalm 23:5

to give out. His desire was for me to be so rested and refreshed that I naturally overflow in every situation. That's true for you, too. That's the miracle of the Sabbath. Simply setting aside one day in seven to recharge and reconnect with God is the key to living in overflow mode.

Your Four Tanks

Please understand, it's not just pastors who are constantly "refueling" others. That's your reality too, no matter what you do for a living. You need fuel to share with your family, people at your job, your friends, and your other relationships. What you do and who you are is so very important to others. There are people who depend on you in a wide variety of ways. As a believer, you carry the light and life of God in you. But you're an ineffective transmitter of that light and life if you're depleted.

The more I thought about that image of a tanker truck, the more I realized how appropriate it is as a metaphor for the believer. Those trucks don't just drive around endlessly. They have to go back to the fuel depot regularly for more fuel. If I am that truck, I, too, must refuel. I need to go back to the fuel depot regularly so that I can continue to fill other people's tanks. I can't give what I don't have. As I pondered that truth, the Lord directly spoke to me again, "Robert, for some reason you've decided that you're wasting time as you 'just sit there doing nothing' while you're refueling back at my fuel depot. You've allowed yourself to feel guilty about a little bit of downtime that is absolutely essential to your ability to continue to supply others."

It was true. I thought about how ridiculous my thinking was in light of the Lord's words to me. Ultimately, I had allowed guilt and peer pressure to gradually pull me away from ever stopping at "the fuel depot." I just kept driving from station to station to station, filling up everyone else's tanks. No wonder I began running on empty! I sputtered along on the shoulder of life's road, headed toward a breakdown.

Since then, I have learned more about how God created us to function in Him. I've discovered that we all have four areas of our lives that become depleted if we don't take the time to rejuvenate and refuel our-selves. It's helpful to think of these four areas as distinct reservoirs, or tanks, that must constantly be refilled to overflowing. You and I have spiritual, physical, emotional, and mental reservoirs. We must regularly refuel all four tanks to make sure we are overflowing for others. How? Through true *rest* as God designed us to experience it.

> You and I have spiritual, physical, emotional, and mental reservoirs.

I've already described how God finally got my attention after five years of trying to constantly refuel others while ignoring God's wise, prescribed method of refueling me. Debbie and I had pushed and pushed in those first five years of Gateway's existence. When you start a new church, you must minister to a wide variety of people in many different ways every day. We just kept going, and going, and going. Some of that "going" included several international mission trips. We traveled vast distances and ministered on the other end of those trips. Often, we witnessed heartbreaking need and devastating tragedy. We poured ourselves out to help in any way we could. But we were already running on fumes.

Every one of our reservoirs was empty. I wasn't replenishing, and she wasn't replenishing. My question is: Are you?

I recall receiving a phone call from a friend that, at first, didn't make a lot of sense to me. The voice on the other end of the line said, "Robert, things are going great for me. Everything's wonderful, actually. But I feel like I'm under attack."

I remember thinking, how do those last two sentences go together? How can you view everything as wonderful, yet still feel like you're under attack? But as I listened further, it became clear to me that my friend was experiencing something quite common. Something I personally recognized from my pre-Sabbath past. I knew from experience that it really is possible to outwardly, objectively be experiencing success, and yet inwardly feel under siege. To feel anxious, floundering, and sad.

When He finished talking, I shared what I knew to be the solution to this problem—the revelation of the four tanks. I told him how we get depleted if we don't take the time to replenish and rejuvenate ourselves in each of those four areas. I told him that, as Christians, our default is to focus on the spiritual tank. Often, we think, "Well, if I just pray a little, I'll get over this." We think that all we have to do is get back to having our quiet time every morning and everything will be fine. Yes, a quiet time is a very beneficial thing, but there are three other tanks that also have to be refilled— a physical tank, an emotional tank, and a mental tank.

In the course of the phone call, I had diagnosed his problem. So, before we hung up, I wrote him a prescription. I said, "When we get off the phone, spend a little time in prayer, take a nap, and then have your family over and watch a funny movie." He promised to follow my instructions to the letter. He texted me later and said, "I can't believe how much better I feel!"

All I did was recommend a few things that would add a little fuel to all four of his tanks. It will work for you, too. You just have to find out what replenishes you. The next time you feel discouraged or like you're under attack, take some time to fill your four tanks. You'll be amazed at how good you'll feel. Let's explore these four tanks as I share some of the things I've found that refill and recharge them.

Your Spiritual Tank

Spending time praying and reading God's Word is the best way to fill your spiritual tank. Unfortunately, these life-giving activities are viewed by many believers as more of an obligatory chore than a nourishing, refreshing privilege. I understand why. If you grew up in church, you've heard all your life that you "ought" to have quiet time every day—around the same time in our lives we were badgered to eat the vegetables we didn't like, do homework we didn't want to finish, and take baths we didn't think we really needed.

In other words, we're conditioned to view "oughts" as unpleasant things, even if we grudgingly acknowledge that they're good for us. It's tragic that time with God and His Word is mentally lumped into that category by so many Christians. The truth is that, like the Sabbath rest itself, it isn't for *His* benefit. Nor is it something that wins us brownie points with Him. It's for *our* enjoyment and benefit.

Charles Stanley has written, "We can be tired, weary, and emotionally distraught, but after spending time alone with God, we find that He injects into our bodies energy, power, and strength."[2] He's right. The fact is, taking time to be alone and still with God isn't a

---

2. Charles Stanley, *How to Listen to God* (Nashville: Thomas Nelson, 2002), 58.

gift to Him. It's a gift to yourself—a very necessary gift. God's Word makes it clear that we're in a daily battle against a very real enemy. There is a reason that the Apostle Paul follows an encouragement to "be strong in the Lord" (in other words, keep your spiritual tank full) with a warning about the spiritual conflict we encounter each day:

> Finally, my brethren, be strong in the Lord and in the power of His might. Put on the whole armor of God, that you may be able to stand against the wiles of the devil. For we do not wrestle against flesh and blood, but against principalities, against powers, against the rulers of the darkness of this age, against spiritual hosts of wickedness in the heavenly places.[3]

Paul follows this advice with the familiar passage about putting on "the whole armor of God." Clearly, Paul understood something that many of us do not. Namely, that we're in a daily war with invisible enemies. They are not "flesh and blood," but rather are "spiritual hosts of wickedness." I don't point this out in order to scare you. Greater is He who is in you than he who is in the world.[4]

> Taking time to be alone and still with God isn't a gift to Him. It's a gift to yourself.

However, you are vulnerable to attack if your spiritual tank is chronically empty. I'm exhorting you the same way Paul exhorted his young protégé: "Timothy, my dear son, *be strong* through the grace that God gives you in Christ Jesus."[5] (emphasis added). I'm encouraging you to

---

3. Ephesians 6:10–12
4. See 1 John 4:4
5. 2 Timothy 2:1 NLT

"be strong" spiritually. And I'm praying for you, dear reader, just as Paul prayed for the believers in Ephesus. I'm asking God:

> ...that He would grant you, according to the riches of His glory, to be strengthened with might through His Spirit in the inner man.[6]

In other words, I'm saying, keep your spiritual tank overflowing! But please remember that it's not your only tank. You have three others.

Your Physical Tank

We live in a culture that is pretty much obsessed with physical fitness. Yet we are the least fit generation in history. We are basically swimming in information and motivation to eat right and to exercise. Yet most of us do neither. And make no mistake about it, when we start talking about taking care of ourselves physically, diet and exercise are the twin pillars of that conversation. Yet there is a third element to physical well-being that goes largely overlooked: rest. There is simply no way to recharge your physical tank without rest.

> There is simply no way to recharge your physical tank without rest.

In her excellent book *Sacred Rest*, medical doctor Saundra Dalton-Smith describes some of the warning indicators of what she calls a "physical rest deficit":

---

6. Ephesians 3:16

- You lack the energy needed to do all of the physical tasks on your to-do list
- You feel tired but you have difficulty falling asleep
- You have a weak immune system with frequent illnesses
- You experience frequent muscle pain and soreness
- You depend on substances to give you more energy (caffeine, energy bars, sugar)
- You depend on substances to give you more rest (alcohol, pills, comfort foods)[7]

Does any of that sound familiar? An avalanche of research in recent years points to the importance of quality sleep for overall health. Chronically bad sleep has now been linked to weight gain, depression, inability to concentrate, low productivity, reduced athletic performance, increased risk of heart attack and stroke, type 2 diabetes risk, diminished immune function, higher levels of inflammation and all the horrible things that go with it, and poorer relationships.[8] Other than that, it's nothing to be concerned about!

Rest in the form of sleep is clearly vital, but there are also certain forms of physical activity that tend to restore you rather than deplete you physically. What those activities are will differ from person to person. For some, it may be taking a walk. For others it might be yard work (not me!). As Dr. Dalton-Smith suggests:

---

7. Saundra Dalton-Smith, *Sacred Rest: Recover Your Life, Renew Your Energy, Restore Your Sanity* (New York: FaithWords, 2017), 41.
8. Joe Leech, "10 Reasons Why Good Sleep Is Important," Healthline, 2018, https://www.healthline.com/nutrition/10-reasons-why-good-sleep-is-important.

Make an effort to find what restores you. Experiment with types of active physical rest to see which produce a deeper level of restfulness, peace, and well-being. What you do *to* your body and what you do *with* your body must balance to maintain equilibrium. We have to stop acting like honoring our body's physical needs is a sign of weakness, period. Rethink your position on body care.[9]

"Well, I don't have time to rest," you may say. Indeed, some of us have difficulty sleeping even when we do have the time. If that's you, I want to encourage you to pray about your situation, turn it over to the Lord, and ask Him to help you find ways to get some rest.

Your Emotional Tank

It probably tells us something about our times that there is an extensive Wikipedia entry for "emotional exhaustion." It points to the fact that we all really do have an emotional tank that can run dry. When it does, we feel numb. We're irritable and find it difficult to handle stressful situations. We tend to find it difficult or impossible to generate enthusiasm, even for things we've enjoyed in the past. We struggle to focus on vital tasks.

The primary fuel for your emotional tank is something the Bible calls *joy*. It's no accident that Psalm 28:7 associates divine joy with strength. C.S. Lewis famously called joy "the serious business of heaven." Far too many of us have allowed stress, time pressure, cares, people-pleasing, etcetera, to crowd out every last measure of joy from

---

9. Dalton-Smith, *Sacred Rest*, 40.

our lives. The famous early twentieth century evangelist Billy Sunday once noted, "If you have no joy, there's a leak in your Christianity somewhere." That leak is in your emotional tank. Or put another way, you're not engaging in the kinds of restful activities that replenish and refill it. For me, it's time with the people I love.

> The primary fuel for your emotional tank is something the Bible calls *joy.*

Recently, our entire family—kids and grandkids—went to the Sea Life Aquarium at a local mall. All the grandkids got to see fish and sharks, and afterward, we went out to eat. We all had a great time, and I came away feeling completely refreshed and engergized. Over the years, I've learned that being around family and friends refreshes me emotionally. It's important to find what works for you.

Your Mental Tank

"Oh, I've just got too much on my mind." That's the common excuse we make to others when we are chronically forgetful, distractible, unfocused, procrastination-prone, accident-prone, or unusually mistake-prone. What you're really revealing when you say something like that is that you've allowed your mental tank to operate on "E."

God created the human mind with an enormous capacity. When healthy, our brains can process amazing amounts of information, synthesize it, draw conclusions from it, and retain it. One Christian counseling textbook from Europe opens a chapter titled "The Miracle of the Human Brain" this way:

TAKE THE DAY OFF

The human brain is the greatest wonder of creation. This little organ weighs only 1500 grams, but contains more nerve cells than there are people on the earth, more than 10 billion, a simply unimaginable number. Each nerve cell is joined to others by hundreds of little offshoots, and the exchange of information between them is brisker than the telephone exchange of a busy capital city. The number of "telephone connections" in one brain exceeds the number of stars in a galaxy. It would be more than 1,000,000,000,000! No computer or telephone exchange is in a position to store and exchange so much information in such a small space as that occupied by the human brain.[10]

You really are carrying a miracle of information management and processing between your ears. But like any other part of your body, soul, or spirit, it will only function as God designed it if you keep it healthy. Rest and restorative activity are the keys to that health.

> Rest and restorative activity are the keys to that health.

You might be surprised to learn that not every book I read has to do with spiritual things, theology, pastoring, or leadership. That wasn't always the case. Just as I used to feel a sense of misplaced guilt for not working on Monday when all my friends were at their jobs, I also felt guilty if I took time to read anything that wasn't directly related to my calling and duties as a minister. What I didn't realize was that when I was reading work-related content at home on my day off, I was basically *working* as opposed to resting. My mind was actively applying everything I

_____

10. Samuel Pfeifer, *Supporting the Weak: Christian Counselling and Contemporary Psychiatry* (Carlisle: Send The Light, 1994), 26.

was reading to the situations and circumstances of my work life. In other words, I was draining my mental tank rather than refilling it.

Fortunately, I'm over that now. I make it a point on my Sabbath days to read things that interest me—things that have no direct relationship to or impact on my workday responsibilities. For me, that includes history—particularly the history of the American West. For example, I recall thoroughly enjoying reading a biography of the remarkable Comanche Indian chief Quanah Parker. At the end of that fascinating reading experience, I felt mentally refreshed and reinvigorated. I read it because it interested me, not because the content had anything to do with my work life.

I've also been delivered from any religious bondage concerning funny movies. I'll admit it. I like watching movies that make me laugh. It's just one of the things that fills my mental tank. Of course, I follow my conscience on inappropriate content. I don't watch anything that defiles my conscience. But there are many very funny movies that I'm comfortable watching with my wife and kids in the room with me. And fortunately, versions of films edited for the airline industry deliver all of the fun with little or none of the inappropriate language or scenes.

I've discovered what works for me. You'll need to do the same. What I know for certain is that you have a mental fuel tank that needs to be regularly topped off. That reality presents a question: How do you know when that is?

Monitor Your Fuel Levels

Literally running out of gas in a car isn't nearly as common as it was when I was a young man carrying a freshly minted driver's license in my wallet. Back then it seemed like I, and other people I knew, ran out of gas with some regularity. And without mobile phones, that meant either hoping an acquaintance would happen to be driving by, or hoofing it to the nearest pay phone or landline. (Readers under a certain age may need to Google the term *pay phone*.)

Why was running out of gas more common back then? Well, for one thing, in small-town East Texas back in the '70s, there wasn't a gas station every two hundred yards as is the case in our urban areas today. Nor did we carry debit cards. We carried cash. And if you didn't have any to carry, you didn't stop for gas. However, I think another technological development is really to be credited for the rarity of getting stranded on the side of the road with an empty gas tank these days.

It's because our gas gauges have gotten so much more sophisticated and accurate. Back in the day, you had little marks on the gauge at the three-quarters, half, and one-quarter full marks. Then there was another mark at E for empty. Of course, everyone knew that E didn't really mean empty. You knew you still had more gas when the needle pointed to E. You just weren't sure *how much* more. It was a guessing game. Not so today. At some point cars became equipped with a "low fuel" light that would come on ominously when you were truly about to run out of gas. Then our gas gauges started telling us exactly how many more miles we could drive until running out. In recent years, car makers have devised ever-more-sophisticated ways of having your car poke, prod, and nag you when you're low on fuel. In other words, we run out of gas far less frequently because our cars have gotten better at monitoring our fuel levels.

When it comes to your four fuel tanks, no flashing "low fuel" light is going to illuminate on your forehead when you're dangerously low in any of those areas. All you have is your own willingness to monitor yourself, along with the Holy Spirit within you, of course. Jesus called Him "the Helper" for a reason. If you let Him, and have a spiritual ear inclined to His voice, He'll let you know. The problem is that when your spiritual tank is low, you're also likely spiritually hard of hearing.

That's why the principle of the Sabbath is so very important. It's the key to staying refreshed and in overflow mode. It's also important to figure out specifically what replenishes those four key areas of your life so you'll know what to do (and avoid) on your Sabbath rest days. What recharges you spiritually, mentally, physically, and emotionally? Many of those things may not seem outwardly spiritual or "holy." That's okay. As long as you're not violating some biblical principle or committing a sin, recharge away! Remember that Paul encouraged us to trust "in the living God, who gives us richly all things to enjoy."[11]

> What recharges you spiritually, mentally, physically, and emotionally?

Read that techno-thriller book. Watch that silly movie. Wet that fishing line. Work that jigsaw puzzle. Hang out with the people who feed your soul and warm your heart. Explore that new exotic restaurant. Sit on your back porch and stare into space. It's all "spiritual" if it recharges and refreshes you.

Let me remind you, the Sabbath isn't a religious chore you have to do so God won't be mad at you. It's a gift God has instructed you to give yourself so you can be His healthy, productive, long-lived representative to a broken world, and accomplish everything He put you on this earth to do. Let's now explore that gift in greater depth.

---

11. 1 Timothy 6:17

CHAPTER FOUR

THE SABBATH WAS
MADE FOR YOU

The Sabbath was made to meet the needs of people, and
not people to meet the requirements of the Sabbath.
—Jesus, (Mark 2:7, NLT)

Any homeowner who's ever undertaken a full kitchen remodel knows
it's one of the most expensive and complex home-improvement projects you can tackle. Even so, Jewish families who want a modern
kitchen but choose to strictly observe the Jewish dietary laws—that is,
to "keep kosher"—have a doubly daunting task before them.

When most of us non-Jews consider the kosher dietary rules, we
think of avoiding pork. Yet, at the heart of creating a kosher kitchen
lies the need to meticulously keep all dairy products away from
meat items. That requires owning two refrigerators. But that's not
all. You also have to keep everything that touches meat away from
everything that touches dairy. So duplicate sets of pots, pans, mix-
ing bowls, and utensils have to not only be kept but also kept separate from one another and easily identified as to which side of the
kitchen they belong. They must never get mixed up. This extends
to having two dishwashers. Even after all the equipment and storage
is in place, keeping kosher still requires strict attention to planning,

scheduling, sequence, and process in food preparation to make sure meat and dairy never become part of the same meal.

Have you ever wondered where in the Old Testament all these complex kosher restrictions came from? Where does it say, "Thou shalt not have a cheeseburger?" Or where is it written, "A bowl that touches chuck roast can never be allowed to touch Monterey Jack?" The answer is, it comes from Exodus 23:19. There God said:

"You must not cook a young goat in its mother's milk."

This eleven-word command is repeated verbatim in Exodus 24:26 and Deuteronomy 14:21. That's it. All of the elaborate kosher regulations about dairy and meat stem from this one small, very specific directive. God basically said, "Don't ever take a young goat and boil it in the milk of its own mother." God doesn't explain *why* he doesn't want them to do this. We can only speculate. It's quite possible that this odd practice was something the local Ammonite or Moabite people did as part of an idolatrous worship ceremony to a false god. Perhaps God saw that the Israelites were being tempted to follow that practice. In fact, we see evidence that this was indeed the case in the instructions God gave them concerning bringing offerings to the Tabernacle. In Leviticus Chapter 17 God tells Moses:

"The reason is so that the sons of Israel may bring their sacrifices which they were sacrificing in the open field, that they may bring them in to the LORD... *They shall no longer sacrifice their sacrifices to the goat demons* with which they play the harlot."[1]

---

1. Leviticus 17:5–7 NASB

Here God personally points out that some among the tribes of Israel were getting caught up in some sort of demonic, goat-centered cult, and they hadn't even entered the land of promise yet! Did playing "the harlot" with these "goat demons" involve a strange ritual feast in which a young goat was boiled in its own mother's milk? If so, that would certainly explain why the Lord repeated the prohibition of the bizarre practice no fewer than three times.

Whatever the reason, we now know that over the centuries the Jewish people expanded, extended, and extrapolated that narrow command into a prohibition involving not just goat meat but *all* meat. And to not just goat's milk from that specific kid's mother, but to *all* dairy products from *all* sources. And to not just boiling, but any form of cooking whatsoever. And to not just cooking meat and dairy together, but even consuming the two within the same meal, even if cooked separately. And to not just cooking and eating, but also to even touching of the same surfaces.

How does that even happen?

I can give you a one-word answer: religion. It's the same impulse that led Adam and Eve to sew fig leaf coverings to hide their shame and compelled the ancient citizens of Babel to try to build a tower to heaven. There is something in the fallen human heart that wants to add to the simple instructions God has given us. Among the people of Israel, that impulse resulted in multiplying and expanding the laws and regulations God gave to them through Moses.

> There is something in the fallen human heart that wants to add to the simple instructions God has given us.

Someone once counted all the commandments and ordinances contained in Exodus, Leviticus, Numbers, and Deuteronomy and came up with 613. You'd think that it would be challenging enough to try to obey 613 specific commands, yet over the centuries, the religious leaders of Israel found ways to expand most of them. By the time Jesus arrived on the scene roughly 1,500 years later, the Pharisees were claiming (falsely) to strictly abide by thousands of rules laid down through oral rabbinic teaching called the *Mishnah*. On one occasion Jesus condemned this expansion of the law by quoting the prophet Isaiah:

> "Thus you have made the commandment of God of no effect by your tradition. Hypocrites! Well did Isaiah prophesy about you, saying: 'These people draw near to Me with their mouth, And honor Me with their lips, But their heart is far from Me. And in vain they worship Me, *Teaching as doctrines the commandments of men.'*"[2] (emphasis added)

On another occasion Jesus condemned these experts on the law, pointing out that although they sternly exhorted the common folks to obey all their made-up rules, they weren't willing to do it themselves:

> "Yes," said Jesus, "what sorrow also awaits you experts in religious law! For you crush people with unbearable religious demands, and you never lift a finger to ease the burden.[3]

Something very similar had happened with God's commandment concerning the Sabbath. Over the centuries many additional restrictions and wrinkles had been added to God's fairly straightforward command to rest on the seventh day. As you read the Gospels, it

---

2. Matthew 15:6–9
3. Luke 11:46 NLT

> Jesus recognized that they'd turned what God meant to be a blessing into a burdensome obligation.

becomes clear that Jesus was always exasperating and infuriating the religious leaders of His day by refusing to abide by all of the extra provisions and restrictions that had been added through the centuries. Jesus recognized that they'd turned what God meant to be a blessing into a burdensome obligation.

In his book, *The Rest of God*, Pastor Mark Buchanan notes that standing between us and experiencing the power of the Sabbath principle are one obstacle and one pitfall. The obstacle is busyness. The pitfall is legalism. He writes:

> For a long while, legalism was the hound that chased Sabbath, kept it gaunt and haunted. That certainly was the situation Jesus met up with in Galilee and thereabouts: the towns jostled with sticklers for the rules, men who studied every nuance of Sabbath rigmarole, who watched every move Jesus made, who whipped themselves into every shade of purple over his infractions. They made a kind of sport of it, devising sting operations to see if they could get Jesus to do something outlandish and, in their eyes, illicit on the Sabbath. He typically obliged, knowing full well what they were doing.[4]

We've already examined the obstacle of busyness. So, it makes sense to now tackle the pitfall to rightly understand how to receive and enjoy the gift of the Sabbath in your life.

---

4. Mark Buchanan, *The Rest of God: Restoring Your Soul by Restoring Sabbath*, Kindle ed. (repr., Nashville, Tennessee: Thomas Nelson, 2006), 106–107.

Life, Not Law

Jesus was home. He was traveling and ministering in the towns and villages encircling the Sea of Galilee—the region where he'd grown from childhood into manhood. He'd also preached, of course, in his home town of Nazareth. But His message repeatedly fell largely on unhearing ears. The seed of the Word found very little receptive soil in these places.

On the back end of this preaching and miracle-working tour of Galilee, we find Jesus in a reflective moment, recorded in the eleventh chapter of Matthew. He begins by pronouncing "woes" upon several of the cities He has just visited. Like an Old Testament prophet, He calls out Capernaum, Chorazin, and Bethsaida and warns that their hard-heartedness would result in impending judgment. Then quite suddenly, Jesus' tone turns gentle and pleading. Was it bondage to religious tradition that kept the people of these cities from receiving Jesus' message? Were they unable to respond to the miracles and glory that Jesus displayed because the legalistic yoke placed upon them by the religious leaders was simply too heavy? I believe so, because the next words that Jesus speaks are these:

"Come to me, all of you who are weary and carry heavy burdens, and I will give you rest. Take my yoke upon you. Let me teach you, because I am humble and gentle at heart, and you will find rest for your souls. For my yoke is easy to bear, and the burden I give you is light."[5]

---

5. Matthew 11:28–30 NLT

One moment Jesus is pronouncing coming woes upon the cities of Galilee, and the next minute He is imploring his listeners to lay down the heavy yokes of legalism

> Lay down the heavy yokes of legalism and take up the light and easy one.

and take up the light and easy one He offered. "Come to me," he invites them, "and I will give you rest."

Rest! It is no coincidence that the next few stories in Matthew's Gospel center around Jesus and the Sabbath—God's designated day of rest for His people. The twelfth chapter of Matthew opens with Jesus and His disciples walking through a grain field on the Sabbath. As they walked, the obviously hungry group picked a few heads of ripe grain from the stalk and ate them. The Pharisees, the self-appointed Law police, were apparently watching from a distance because they immediately pulled Jesus over and tried to write Him a citation:

> And when the Pharisees saw it, they said to Him, "Look, Your disciples are doing what is not lawful to do on the Sabbath!"[6]

Jesus responds by pointing them to an Old Testament incident involving no less a figure than David:

> But He said to them, "Have you not read what David did when he was hungry, he and those who were with him: how he entered the house of God and ate the showbread which was not lawful for him to eat, nor for those who were with him, but only for the priests? Or have you not read in the law that on the Sabbath the priests in the temple profane the Sabbath, and are blameless?[7]

6. Matthew 12:2
7. Matthew 12:3–5

Citing these examples would have been enough to send the Pharisees into a rage because they involved Jesus—a carpenter from some backwater town in what they considered hillbilly country—comparing Himself to the great King David. But Jesus wasn't finished ruffling their religious feathers:

> "Yet I say to you that in this place there is One greater than the temple. But if you had known what this means, 'I desire mercy and not sacrifice,' you would not have condemned the guiltless. For the Son of Man is Lord even of the Sabbath."[8]

Here Jesus reveals something to the Pharisees that He had taken great pains to conceal from others: *He is the Messiah.* For these experts on the writings of the Law and the Prophets, the terms "One greater than the temple" and "Lord even of the Sabbath" are both clear pronouncements. Jesus is telling them plainly that He is the long-awaited Savior of God's people. Of course, they didn't believe Him. Such a claim only sent their anger soaring.

In Mark's account of this same incident, he records one additional sentence in Jesus' words to the Pharisees. Right before declaring Himself to be the "Lord even of the Sabbath," Jesus said:

> "The Sabbath was made for man, and not man for the Sabbath."[9]

In one simple sentence, Jesus identified the fatal flaw in the legalistic, religious mind-set. In twelve words, He explained where the rabbis and lawyers had gone wrong over the centuries. Somewhere

8. Matthew 12:6–8
9. Mark 2:27

along the way they had turned God's purpose for the principle of the Sabbath on its head.

They had begun demanding that God's people serve the Sabbath, instead of encouraging them to allow the Sabbath to serve them.

You weren't made for the Sabbath. It was made for you. The Sabbath is a gift. God didn't create people so there would finally be creatures on the planet who would honor His Sabbath. He created the Sabbath as a gift to His beloved People. This statement was both a bombshell revelation and an outrage to the Pharisees listening to Jesus' words. But the conversation wasn't over yet. Matthew reveals that Jesus then headed toward the local synagogue. There the Pharisees set up a test to see just how far Jesus would go in violating their distorted sense of what was permissible on the Sabbath.

> You weren't made for the Sabbath. It was made for you.

Now when He had departed from there, He went into their synagogue. And behold, there was a man who had a withered hand. And they asked Him, saying, "Is it lawful to heal on the Sabbath?"—that they might accuse Him.

Then He said to them, "What man is there among you who has one sheep, and if it falls into a pit on the Sabbath, will not lay hold of it and lift it out? Of how much more value then is a man than a sheep? Therefore it is lawful to do good on the Sabbath." Then He said to the man, "Stretch out your hand." And he stretched it out, and it was restored as whole as the other.[10]

---

10. Matthew 12:9–13

Here we see the clash between what legalism values and what God values. Legalism loves the system. God loves people.

> Legalism loves the system. God loves people.

What was the Pharisees' response to this act of compassion? Did they rejoice with the man and his family? Did they repent and adjust their paradigm, given that the miracle-working power of God had just endorsed what Jesus had said? Uh, not exactly:

> Then the Pharisees went out and immediately plotted with the Herodians against Him, how they might destroy Him.[11]

There is a remarkable element in the sentence above that tends to go right over our heads unless we understand the politics and culture of Jesus' day. Namely, the fact that the Pharisees and the Herodians despised one another. They were mortal enemies in that time. The Herodians were Jewish compromisers. They were the elite of Jewish society in Judea and Galilee who were willing to set aside many of their religious convictions in exchange for privileges and prestige from the occupying Roman Empire. They chose to go along to get along. And to the ultrasticklers, the Pharisees, this was nothing short of betrayal of Abraham, Moses, and David. Even, so the Pharisees were so offended by Jesus and His rejection of what they believed about the Sabbath (the fourth commandment), they were willing to cooperate with the despised rival in plotting Jesus' death and thereby violate the sixth commandment (prohibiting murder)!

Jesus understood what they clearly did not. The Sabbath is not a

---

11. Mark 3:6

rigid, inflexible, complex set of restrictions to be followed. It's really an invitation to be accepted.

As I discovered on my first-ever visit to Israel, keeping the Sabbath (Shabbat) remains serious business to this day. On that first trip, we'd been staying in one of the upper floors of a Jerusalem hotel for several days when Friday evening rolled around. That night I entered the elevator to head up to my room, pushed the button for my floor, and…nothing happened. I pushed it again, and once again, nothing happened. I remember turning to one of my traveling companions and saying, "The elevator's broken." Then the light came on for both of us: "It's Friday and the sun has set. It's the Sabbath!" I knew that, according to the strict Shabbat regulations, even pressing an elevator button is considered "work." I recall thinking, "So it's considered 'work' for me to press an elevator button, but it's not 'work' for me to walk up eight flights of stairs?" Actually, like most multistory buildings in Israel, one elevator remains in operation that automatically stops on every floor throughout Shabbat. That way, no one has to violate the Sabbath by pressing a button.

"Where in the Bible does this ban on button pushing come from," you ask? Like the kosher wall between meat and cheese, it can be traced back to a much simpler, straightforward command. In Exodus 35, while repeating His instruction on honoring the Sabbath, God says, "You shall kindle no fire throughout your dwellings on the Sabbath day." Through the centuries, that "no fire building" rule was extended to include a "no lighting of lamps" rule. And then when electricity in homes became common, this translated into a "no turning lights on" rule. Now, in the age of smart, internet-connected appliances, most new refrigerators come with a Shabbat-mode option. Enable that option and the interior light of your refrigerator won't come on during the hours of the Sabbath.

That's right. Even allowing a light to come on that you don't actually turn on is considered a prohibited activity on the Sabbath. As a result, observant households with an older refrigerator will remove the bulb on Friday afternoon and replace it on Saturday night.

Are you beginning to see how creeping legalism can choke all the life and blessing out of God's amazing gift of the Sabbath? I'm not singling out my observant Jewish friends and neighbors here. Some of my fellow Christians have done the same thing. I've seen mature believers slide into legalism about any number of things that are good, in and of themselves. We're all capable of giving in to the religious impulse. When we do, we lose the blessing God intends us to experience when we obey from the heart, rather than from mere outward observance of man-made rules.

When we embrace God's principles from the heart, it's not law. It's life!

Are You Ready to Flourish?

God never intended us to become rigid and legalistic about our day of rest. He gave the Sabbath to us as a loving Father to bless His children. It is a joy to rest. And there is great power and strength to be gained from pausing once a week to fellowship with God—to find refreshment and renewal as we contemplate his goodness and might. That is precisely the message of one of our most loved Psalms. In the New King James translation, the 92nd psalm carries the heading: "A Song for the Sabbath Day." It opens with these words:

> Find refreshment and renewal as we contemplate his goodness and might.

It is good to give thanks to the Lord,
And to sing praises to Your name, O Most High;
To declare Your lovingkindness in the morning,
And Your faithfulness every night.[12]

Here the psalmist declares his attitude about the Sabbath: it is a day for honoring the Lord and singing praises to Him. What is the result of this? A few verses later, the psalmist lets us know: "I have been anointed with fresh oil."[13] Please take note of that. Pausing for a day to be grateful and think about God's love and faithfulness resulted in the writer receiving a fresh anointing from God. This is a far bigger deal than many Christians realize. This covering of anointing oil upon a person is a metaphor for the Spirit of God resting upon a person.

Receiving an "anointing" from the Spirit of God isn't just churchy lingo for feeling closer to God. It isn't a warm, fuzzy feeling that has no real impact on your daily life. If you doubt me, do a study through the Old Testament on the men and women who are said to have the Spirit of God resting upon them. In Exodus it was a special anointing of the Spirit that gave artists and artisans among the Israelites supernatural gifting to craft the materials for the Tabernacle.[14] It was the Spirit that equipped Joshua to lead and conquer. It was the Spirit that filled Samson with the strength of many men.[15] In First Samuel Chapter 16 we learn: "Then Samuel took the horn of oil and anointed him in the midst of his brothers; and the Spirit of the Lord came upon David from that day forward." David's authority and gifting

---

12. Psalm 92:1–2
13. Psalm 92:10
14. See Exodus 28:3, 31:3, 35:31
15. See Judges 14:6

to rule Israel came the day Samuel anointed him and the Spirit of God came upon him. Keep in mind that this is the Old Covenant era. These people weren't even born again. You and I have the huge advantage of not only having the Spirit of God upon us, but within us! Nevertheless, Paul wouldn't have exhorted us to continually "be filled with the Spirit" if we didn't need regular "fill-ups" for our tanks.

Please don't undervalue a fresh anointing of the Spirit of God. It can and will equip you to accomplish more in six days than you can do in sixteen days in your own strength. It can make you more creative, more insightful, more focused, more intuitive, and just plain old stronger than you could ever be on your own. If you're not regularly operating in this supernatural level of performance and ability, perhaps you're not receiving regular, fresh anointings. And maybe that is because you've neglected the pathway that God designated for you to receive your refills—the Sabbath! Yet this is not the only benefit described by the 92nd psalm. Verse 12 tells us:

The righteous shall flourish like a palm tree.

And verse 14 reveals:

They shall still bear fruit in old age; They shall be fresh and flourishing.

Why would this be? Why would righteous people still be fresh, flourishing, and fruit bearing, even in old age? Could it be because they willingly received God's restorative gift of the Sabbath? Who doesn't want to flourish? I know I do! How

> Who doesn't want to flourish? I know I do!

79

about riding on the heights of the earth? Does that sound fun? Well, according to Isaiah 58, that is precisely what you will do if you honor God's wisdom for your life by making the Sabbath a priority. There, God says:

> "If because of the sabbath, you turn your foot
> From doing your own pleasure on My holy day,
> And call the sabbath a delight, the holy day of the LORD
>   honorable,
> And honor it, desisting from your own ways,
> From seeking your own pleasure
> And speaking your own word,
> Then you will take delight in the LORD,
> And I will make you ride on the heights of the earth;
> And I will feed you with the heritage of Jacob your father,
> For the mouth of the LORD has spoken."[16]

This passage represents a wonderful promise for all believers willing to take a step of faith and embrace the principle of the Sabbath. "Step" is exactly the right word here because the Lord begins by talking about turning your *foot* from doing your own thing. That's exactly what honoring the Sabbath requires. A hundred different things are clamoring for your attention. Your natural impulse—"your own pleasure"—is to attend to those things. If you're a workaholic, "your own pleasure" is to be working. But the wise person steps away.

The Lord follows that by encouraging us to "call the Sabbath a delight." The Hebrew translated "delight" carries the meaning of "a luxury." The attitude God is encouraging here is for us to view

---

16. Isaiah 58:13, 14 NASB

the Sabbath as a luxury. Something special rather than common. Something to look forward to, rather than dread. We have a stunted, distorted view of our generous God if we believe that He wants to offer us less on *His* holy day than we can offer ourselves. The Sabbath is a gift and our observance of it is a bold declaration of our trust in God's goodness and ability to provide what we need—heart, mind, and body.

> The Sabbath is a gift and our observance of it is a bold declaration of our trust in God's goodness and ability to provide what we need.

Please notice that turning aside and delighting in the Sabbath brings a great reward. Isaiah says if you do this, "then you will take delight in the Lord." Sometimes I hear from Christians who say something along the lines of, "I really envy your intimate relationship with God. It seems like you and the Father have such a close, special connection. He speaks so clearly to you. I wish we had that kind of relationship." Can I tell you something? I'm not special. This passage makes it clear. If you want to take more delight in your relationship with the Lord, turn your foot aside from doing your own, busy thing and embrace the Sabbath. "Then," the Word promises us, "you will take delight in the Lord." Or as the New King James translates that verse:

"Then you shall delight yourself in the Lord;
And I will cause you to ride on the high hills of the earth,
And feed you with the heritage of Jacob your father.
The mouth of the Lord has spoken."[17]

---

17. Isaiah 58:14

Does that phrase, "delight yourself in the Lord," remind you of another verse in the Bible? Most believers are familiar with the words of Psalm 37:4: "Delight yourself also in the Lord, And He shall give you the desires of your heart." Many people have read that verse and wondered, "How? How do I delight myself in the Lord?" In other words, "How can I get to a place where God really is my delight, if I don't sincerely feel that way?" Now you know the answer to that question. The Sabbath is your gateway to being that kind of person. And what is the result? The Lord will "cause you to ride on the high hills of the earth!"

CHAPTER FIVE

TREAT YOURSELF

Rejoice in Christ Jesus, for in Him you are complete.
His righteousness is over you, His strong arm is around
you...This is a safe place to rest in.

—James Hamilton

In the opening pages of this book I pointed out that we're experiencing an epidemic of sleep trouble in our culture, and that poor sleep is at the root of a wide array of other physical, mental, and emotional disorders.

Well, have you ever noticed that the Jewish Sabbath begins at sundown? In fact, God has always reckoned the day to begin with the evening. Right there in the beginning of the creation account in Genesis 1:3 the Word says, "God called the light Day, and the darkness He called Night. *So the evening and the morning were the first day.*" We think our day begins at sunrise. But God says it begins at sunset.

This is especially true concerning the Sabbath. In observant Jewish households around the world, Friday afternoon is a busy time of preparation for the rapidly approaching twenty-four hours of Sabbath inactivity that will begin with the setting of the sun. Meals are prepared in advance. Chores are preemptively attended to.

Everything is set in order because the family knows that the setting of the sun brings a celebratory meal, and then rest. In fact, before the age of electric lighting in homes, most people simply went to bed shortly after it got dark.

That's right. The Sabbath begins with nourishment and then sleep. Do you see what God is trying to say about the Sabbath through this pattern? When you are asleep, you aren't striving, planning, managing, creating, building, or fixing. You aren't in control of anything. You are most vulnerable when you're sleeping. In other words, you have to trust God completely when you sleep.

Let me repeat one more time…the Sabbath is a step of faith. A fundamental element of the Sabbath rest is relaxing in trust and confidence in God's goodness and faithfulness. When you do, your sleep is deep, sound, replenishing, and restorative. Or as wise King Solomon, the author of Proverbs, put it…"sweet!"

When you lie down, you will not be afraid; Yes, you will lie down and your sleep will be sweet. Do not be afraid of sudden terror, Nor of trouble from the wicked when it comes; For the LORD will be your confidence.[1]

> In sleeping you're modeling the posture you should have throughout the Sabbath day… safe and secure in the loving arms of a good, good Father.

God has you begin your day of rest with a good night's sleep because in sleeping you're modeling the posture you should have throughout the Sabbath day. Relaxed. At peace. Trusting. Confident. Safe and secure

1. Proverbs 3:24–26

in the loving arms of a good, good Father. David had this state of relaxation in mind when he wrote:

> LORD, my heart is not proud; my eyes are not haughty.
> I don't concern myself with matters too great or too awesome
>   for me to grasp.
> Instead, I have calmed and quieted myself, like a weaned
>   child who no longer cries for its mother's milk.
> Yes, like a weaned child is my soul within me.[2]

"Sweet" sleep requires absolute trust in God. Have you ever had a problem with going to sleep? Or awakened in the night with your mind racing so you can't fall back to sleep? I have, and I can tell you why—I wasn't trusting God. Deep in my mind and heart (my soul) I still believed I had to take care of things—to find solutions to my problems.

I am married to a wonderful woman who can sleep anywhere, anytime, anyplace, instantly. Sometimes, we'll be lying in bed talking or reading and she'll say to me, "I'm a little tired. I'd like to go to sleep."

I say, "That's great honey. I love you. I'll see you in the morning."

And before I even finish my sentence, I hear, "Zzz." *Really? She's already gone!* One night, she was lying there sleeping, and I was lying next to her doing what I thought was the *responsible* thing: worrying. We had been discussing some financial decisions we were facing as a couple, and I was a little put out because she was now sleeping peacefully while I thought she should have been up worrying with me. Of course, in that moment I wouldn't have admitted to

---

2. Psalm 131:1, 2 NLT

"worrying." In my mind, I was simply being a responsible problem solver. I continued to go over and over things in my mind, searching for plans, ideas, and solutions. There is a part of me (a prideful part) that believes I can find a way to fix everything that is broken or wrong. Me. Personally.

I don't believe I'm alone in that. We're all constantly telling ourselves a story in which we are the hero.

Now, Debbie and I are a traditional couple when it comes to our roles in the marriage. Throughout our entire relationship, Debbie has managed the home and I have managed the finances. The reason for that arrangement is that it is in alignment with our God-given giftings. I'm a numbers guy. I inherited that from my father. Managing the budget and our expenses comes naturally for me. Debbie would hate it. Yet, we know a number of couples where the wife is more gifted and equipped in that area and she oversees the budget and tracks spending. Responsibility should follow gifting. That's why, at our house, the responsibility for the finances has always fallen to me.

She will tell you that she has never spent a single day worrying about our finances. She usually doesn't know where we are financially. It's not because I don't tell her. I do. It's not that she's not intelligent. As anyone who knows us will testify, she's far smarter than I am. It's simply because she doesn't take the care of it. Not one bit. A special offering at the church will be approaching, so over breakfast I'll say to her, "How much do you think we should give?"

She'll say, "Um, fifty thousand!"

"What?!" I respond while mopping up spewed coffee from the breakfast table. "Do you really think we have that much money?"

She'll say, "I have no idea! Okay, five thousand? Ten? Whatever. Just do whatever you believe the Lord wants us to do. I trust you."

That's our thing. I've taken care of the money, so she's completely relaxed about it.

So, on this particular night I was lying in bed stewing while she was sleeping. I was finding myself fuming because we were clearly facing a situation in which I felt we *both* should be worrying about money. I was thinking to myself, "How can she be sleeping so peacefully? I know how. She can sleep because of *me*. She doesn't have a worry in the world because she has a husband that takes care of her. Must be nice!"

In that moment, I heard the familiar inward voice of the Lord ask, "Why can't you sleep, Robert?"

Still feeling like a martyr, I replied, "Because *I* don't have a husband that takes care of me."

As soon as those words were formed and expressed in my mind, I sensed they had deeply grieved the Father's heart. He said, "Really? May I remind you Robert, that I take care of you better than you take care of her? My Word says I'm your husband, you're My bride. If you trusted Me like she trusts you, you could go to sleep, too."

He was right, of course. I was carrying burdens I wasn't meant to carry. Lying awake wrestling with my problems and striving to come up with solutions from my own puny, finite brain revealed a stunning absence of trust in God's faithfulness, and a forgetfulness of His immense power. I repented, rolled my cares over onto a faithful, powerful Father who loves me more than I could possibly imagine, and drifted off to sleep.

If you're having difficulty sleeping, it might be because you don't trust God to take care of you. Your mind is too busy working on solutions to all your problems and plotting pathways to all your goals—which brings me back to my point about how the Sabbath begins with the evening. The same posture and attitude that make

> The same posture and attitude that make for a good night's sleep also make for a truly restful Sabbath.

for a good night's sleep also make for a truly restful Sabbath. First and foremost, it requires trust in your heavenly Father.

Think about it. What keeps you from totally shutting down for a full day once each week in accordance with the principle of the Sabbath? What thoughts go through your mind as you contemplate doing that? You might think, "If I take a day off, everything will fall apart!" "I'll lose all my momentum." "My competitors will get ahead of me." Or, "Bad things will happen if I'm not vigilantly monitoring everything." If you're honest with yourself, you might find that you simply don't trust that God is up to the task of handling things while you're not working. My friend, either God's in control or He is not. Either a good God is working all things together for your good or He's not. Either Jesus is "Lord of All" or you are. Which is it?

Recall how the author of Hebrews interpreted the story of the Israelites' wilderness wanderings. They could not enter God's rest—the promised land of abundance and security—because of their unbelief. Let me give you another word for unbelief. Mistrust. They didn't trust God to give them victory if they just did things His way. How about you? Do you trust God to provide what you need if you embrace His way of doing things? Do you trust God to give you the desires of your heart? The fact is, God cares deeply about both your needs and your wants. At the same time, God's Word is very clear about the fact that worry and care have no appropriate place in the heart of a believer. For example, First Peter 5:6–7 tells us:

Therefore humble yourselves under the mighty hand of God, that He may exalt you in due time, casting all your care upon Him, for He cares for you.

Notice the role of humility in the verse above. One major obstacle to entering the rest of the Sabbath is pride. There is something in fallen human nature that wants to do everything on its own. We want to be able to say, much like a boastful six-year-old who has just mastered shoe tying, "I did this all by myself!" We don't want to feel dependent. Yet we *are* dependent. That's reality. Paul said that in God "...we live and move and have our being."[3] Jesus couldn't have made this clearer when He said, "I am the vine, you are the branches. He who abides in Me, and I in him, bears much fruit; for without Me you can do nothing."[4] Anything of lasting value you ever do will be done through your living, breathing connection to the Life of God through His Son, Jesus Christ. That's what makes our refusal to trust God in every area of our lives—including our work lives—so wrong-headed and tragic.

Entering into the blessings of Sabbath rest means both humbly recognizing your need for God *and* trusting that He does indeed care for you. Because both things are true, you can freely cast your worries on Him and receive. Jesus said,

"Therefore do not worry, saying, 'What shall we eat?' or 'What shall we drink?' or 'What shall we wear?' For after all these things the Gentiles seek. For your heavenly Father

---

3. Acts 17:28
4. John 15:5

knows that you need all these things. But seek first the kingdom of God and His righteousness, and all these things shall be added to you. Therefore do not worry about tomorrow, for tomorrow will worry about its own things. Sufficient for the day is its own trouble."[5]

> Trust. Believe. Sleep sweetly. Rest deeply.

Trust. Believe. Sleep sweetly. Rest deeply. You can because the God who loves you is faithful, good, and strong.

Three Reasons to Rest

Something happened in 2016 that had not occurred in the United States in one hundred years. Then it happened again in 2017.

For two years in a row, the average life expectancy in America dropped.[6] Throughout most of our history, the United States has enjoyed ever-increasing average life spans. We've also led the world in expected longevity. Not even the deprivations of the Great Depression or the appalling death tolls of World War II could dent the upward climb of Americans' life expectancy figures. But no longer.

Yes, after roughly two centuries of continual increases,[7] the US average life expectancy dropped in 2016, and again in 2017, down

5. Matthew 6:31–34

6. Grace Donnelly, "Here's Why Life Expectancy in the U.S. Dropped Again This Year," *Fortune*, 2018, http://fortune.com/2018/02/09/us-life-expectancy-dropped-again/.

7. "Life Expectancy by Age, 1850–2011," Infoplease, accessed 25 June 2019, https://www.infoplease.com/us/mortality/life-expectancy-age-1850-2011.

to 78.7 years—a full year and a half lower than that of nations like the UK, Germany, Canada, France, Mexico, and Japan. We're going the wrong way.[8] What caused this stunning reversal? A report by the British Medical Journal points to two causes: an epidemic of addiction to opioid painkillers, and "despair."[9] That's right. *Despair.* The author of the study considered it "alarming" that "addiction and the decline in the emotional wellbeing of Americans have been significant enough to drag down the country's average length of life."[10]

I find that alarming, too. As I've pointed out, we're suffering from an epidemic of weariness in our nation. We're running ourselves to death. And it's not just physical exhaustion that's killing us. As this study reveals, we're emotionally and mentally spent as well. When I see that pain-killing drugs and "despair" are actually shortening our life spans as a people, I can't help but think of Jesus' plea for the weary and heavy-laden to come to Him. What did He promise those who would come to Him?

Rest for our souls!

Have you ever worked long hours, day after day, for weeks at a time, without ever stopping to rest? As I've already confessed, I have. And invariably, I would eventually become sick. My immune system would become compromised and I'd end up flat on my back for several days. In effect, my body was forcing me to pay back the rest of which I'd been robbing it. God is serious about rest because He is serious about you. He loves you, and He designed you.

---

8. "Life Expectancy by Age."

9. Steven H. Woolf and Laudan Aron, "Failing Health of the United States," BMJ.com, 2018, https://www.bmj.com/content/360/bmj.k496.

10. Abby Haglage, "U.S. Life Expectancy Has Fallen Again. Here Are Three Reasons Why," Yahoo, 2018, https://sg.news.yahoo.com/u-s-life-expectancy-keeps -dropping-alcohol-blame-185004863.html.

TAKE THE DAY OFF

The fact is, there are three keys reasons we should trust God
and embrace a Sabbath rest by setting aside one day each week—
whatever day works best for you—for complete and total recharging and renewal. Let's examine each of those three reasons now.

1. A Sabbath gives God the opportunity to provide for us supernaturally.

We see this vividly illustrated with the Israelites in the book of
Exodus.

In Exodus Chapter 16 we find the account of how the Lord
began to sustain His people by providing manna in the wilderness.
As you may recall, with this miraculous provision came some specific instructions. Each morning, when a fresh batch of the heavenly
food appeared on the ground around the Israelite camp, they were to
only gather enough to provide for their family for that day. Anyone
who attempted to save some of that day's provision found that it had
become putrid and wormy by the next day. One lesson here is that
God wants us to trust Him and have confidence in His ability to
provide. Trying to save some of that day's manna was a clear indicator that a person didn't trust God to do it again the next day.

The command to only gather one day's provision of manna did
present a challenge on Friday. After all, the Israelites were forbidden to work or gather on the Sabbath. And if gathering sticks on
the Sabbath carried the death penalty, then gathering manna would
have been off the table as well. Of course, that didn't catch God by
surprise:

Then he said to them, "This is what the LORD has said:
'Tomorrow is a Sabbath rest, a holy Sabbath to the LORD.

Bake what you will bake today, and boil what you will boil; and lay up for yourselves all that remains, to be kept until morning.'" So they laid it up till morning, as Moses commanded; and it did not stink, nor were there any worms in it. Then Moses said, "Eat that today, *for today is a Sabbath to the* LORD; *today you will not find it in the field. Six days you shall gather it, but on the seventh day, the Sabbath, there will be none.*"[11] (emphasis added)

If God had provided manna on the Sabbath day, He would have essentially been inviting His people to violate His own law. God would never do that. Instead, He instructed them to gather two days' worth of manna on Friday, and then miraculously kept the manna fresh and nutritious throughout the second day. Here's another lesson for you and me: we shouldn't expect God's supernatural help if we're working seven days a week. If we're going to ignore the Sabbath, we won't find miraculous help, provision, favor, or increase on that seventh day. But if we honor the principle of the Sabbath, we'll find miraculous help on the other six days, and even a double portion of help on the sixth!

> If we honor the principle of the Sabbath, we'll find miraculous help on the other six days, and even a double portion of help on the sixth!

Wouldn't you know, that even after God miraculously gave them a double portion on Friday, they still went out on the Sabbath to try to gather more? Just as God had told them, they found none. They violated God's command for nothing. In the process, they

---

11. Exodus 16:23–26

outed themselves as being both greedy and untrusting of God. Not surprisingly, God was not amused and exhorted Moses to explain His instructions so clearly that even a hardhead could understand them:

> And the LORD said to Moses, "How long do you refuse to keep My commandments and My laws? See! *For the* LORD *has given you the Sabbath*; therefore He gives you on the sixth day bread for two days. Let every man remain in his place; let no man go out of his place on the seventh day."[12] (emphasis added)

Please note the words in italics in the passage above: "For the Lord has given you the Sabbath." God was exasperated because the Sabbath was His *gift* to the people and they were refusing to receive it. God was basically saying, "Take the day off! Please! I'm going to provide double for you on Friday so you can rest properly on the Sabbath!"

Today, honoring and integrating the principle of the Sabbath into your life gives God an opportunity to show you what He can and will do on your behalf. I can tell you from personal experience and from the testimonies of many believers, if you trust Him by shutting down completely one day each week, you'll find God supernaturally providing and blessing on the six remaining days.

Allow me to repeat a key truth. This is very similar to the way tithing works. I've discovered I'd much rather have 90 percent of my income with God's blessing on it than 100 percent without His blessing. Having God's blessing on my finances and on the material things over which I exercise stewardship is so powerful. I've

---

12. Exodus 16:28, 29

heard countless people say, "I can't afford to tithe." And I always reply, "I've learned that I can't afford *not* to tithe!" The same thing is true with your time. Embracing God's principle of the Sabbath by unplugging for a day invites His supernatural blessing on your remaining six days. God can accomplish far more in six days that carry God's supernatural blessing than you can in seven without it.

How much can God do in six days? Look around. Look up on a clear night away from the lights of the city. This extraordinary planet and the unimaginably vast universe in which it hangs were created by your heavenly Father in six days. Don't ever doubt what God's blessing on your six workdays can do.

> How much can God do in six days?

What's true for individuals is also true for business enterprises. The Chick-fil-A restaurant chain defies all fast-food industry conventional wisdom by closing their stores on Sunday. Closing on Sunday, the day when many families eat out, is unthinkable for most food chains. In fact, to maximize per-store sales, many are staying open twenty-four hours a day. Founded by a Christian family headed by a born-again believer, the late S. Truett Cathy, Chick-fil-A has stubbornly refused to open their stores on Sunday. Here's how Chick-fil-A explains that decision on the company's website:

> Our founder, Truett Cathy, made the decision to close on Sundays in 1946 when he opened his first restaurant in Hapeville, Georgia. Having worked seven days a week in restaurants open 24 hours, Truett saw the importance of closing on Sundays so that he and his employees could set aside one day to rest and worship if they choose—a practice we uphold today.

In spite of what the restaurant industry views as a disadvantage, the company's growth and success continue to stun the business world. A 2017 article on the popular business website *Business Insider* put it this way:

> Chick-fil-A is dominating fast food.
>
> The company generates more revenue per restaurant than any other fast-food chain in the US, and it's only open six days a week.
>
> Chick-fil-A has only 2,100 restaurants, and none of its restaurants are open on Sundays. For comparison, McDonald's has more than 14,100 locations in the US, Taco Bell has nearly 6,300, and KFC has more than 4,160—most of which are open seven days a week.
>
> Yet, Chick-fil-A generates more annual revenue than dozens of other chains that have more than twice as many US locations, including KFC, Pizza Hut, Domino's, and Arby's.[13]

That's right. Even with far fewer restaurant locations, Chick-fil-A restaurants do far more business in six days than most of their competitors do in seven. Imagine that! An even better way to measure how much more productive Chick-fil-A stores are than the rest of the industry is to calculate average annual sales per restaurant. This evens the playing field with chains that have many more locations. The same article reported that in 2016, the average sales per restaurant for Chick-fil-A was $4.4 million. By comparison, its most

---

13. Hayley Peterson, "Why Chick-Fil-A's Restaurants Sell 4 Times as Much as KFC's," *Business Insider*, 2017, https://www.businessinsider.com/why-chick-fil-a-is-so-successful-2017-8.

similar competitor, KFC, generated $1.1 million per restaurant in that same time period.[14]

That's exactly four times as much revenue per outlet with one less day per week. Please don't try to convince me that six days with God's blessing on it isn't far better than seven days of effort without it. You're too late. I've seen the results!

God is pleading with us, "Trust me! Just watch what I can do through you if you'll embrace my principles and my ways." The Sabbath gives God an opportunity to provide for us supernaturally. But that's not all.

2. The Sabbath gives us the opportunity to rest and be refreshed.

In the thirty-first chapter of Exodus we find a remarkable statement concerning the reason for resting on the Sabbath:

> Therefore the children of Israel shall keep the Sabbath, to observe the Sabbath throughout their generations as a perpetual covenant. It is a sign between Me and the children of Israel forever; for in six days the LORD made the heavens and the earth, and on the seventh day He rested and was refreshed.' "[15]

First, please notice that God declares the observance of the Sabbath to be a "perpetual covenant." *Perpetual* means there's no expiration date on it. And covenant means that not only is the Sabbath

---

14. Peterson, "Why Chick-Fil-A's Restaurants Sell 4 Times as Much as KFC's."
15. vv. 16–17

a command designed to help them prosper as a society, it's also a marker of the solemn agreement God is making with the Israelites as a people. What is that agreement? If you'll remember your connection to and dependence on Me by observing the Sabbath, I'll supernaturally help and bless you. This explains God's next statement about the Sabbath. He says it's to be "a sign" between Himself and them forever. What do signs do? They signify (sign-ify) something. The Israelites' weekly day of rest would signify their covenantal relationship with God—not only to themselves, but to the other nations of the world. The Sabbath would mark and separate God's people. Yes, the Israelites carried another sign of their covenant with Him, but that one wasn't visible to the people of other cultures: circumcision. Sabbath is a visible sign to the whole world!

Most importantly, faithful Sabbath observance would serve as a sign to future generations of Israelites—generations that would one day inhabit the land of promise and would not have witnessed the wonders of their deliverance from Egypt or have experienced miraculous provision in the wilderness. Those generations would need a constant reminder, a sign, that they were in a sacred agreement with God through which He promised to care for them if only they would trust Him. At some point in the life of every Israelite child— perhaps around the inquisitive age of four or five when every other word seems to be "Why?"—he or she would ask a parent why they always spent Friday afternoon preparing to be idle for twenty-four hours; or on Saturday, "Why don't you cook today, Mama?" This would give every parent an opportunity to explain their covenant with God and talk about His faithfulness and power. Yes, as God declares in this passage, the Sabbath was to be a sign. But notice what else he says about it.

It's a sign that points them back to God, and to His six days of creation activity. God declares the Sabbath to be a sign between Him and Israel forever. Why?

> "...for in six days the Lord made the heavens and the earth, and on the seventh day He rested and was refreshed."

That's a pretty startling statement there. We've always heard that God "rested" on the seventh day. It's challenging to ponder the fact that God rested. We know God doesn't get tired or worn out. In fact, God explicitly tells us in Isaiah 40:28 that, "The Creator of the ends of the earth, neither faints nor is weary." But it's not hard to understand that the word "rest" here means that God simply ceased His creation activity. He was finished. He'd been active for six creation days, but now everything He'd planned to do was complete. He looked around and declared it "good." God rested, or ceased creating, after six days.

But what about that word "refreshed"? If our omnipotent God doesn't get weary or depleted, in what sense could He possibly ever be refreshed? We'll find the answer in the Hebrew word that English translators render "refreshed." It's the word *naphash* and it literally means "to breathe in," or, "to take a breath." In the two other places this word appears in the Old Testament, it refers to a place or moment in which humans can, in modern terms, stop to catch their breath.

> It refers to a place or moment in which humans can, in modern terms, stop to catch their breath.

God never gets out of breath. Even so, the use of this word makes perfect sense in the light of what Genesis tells us about God's six-day burst of creative activity. How did God create light, the world, and all the world contains? He *spoke* them into existence. Speaking involves exhalation, or outward breathing. And when it came time to make mankind in His own image and likeness, Genesis 2:7 tells us: "And the Lord God formed man of the dust of the ground, *and breathed into his nostrils the breath of life*; and man became a living being" (KJV)

For the six days of creation God had been breathing out. Now, on the seventh day, it was time to *naphash*—to breathe in.

Here is my question for you: If God refreshed Himself, why don't you? If the mighty Creator of heaven and earth paused to breathe, why would you or I ever think we can get away with not following His example? It's no accident that in the same moment God is reminding His people to observe the Sabbath, He's pointing out that He did the same thing. And that in doing so, He was refreshed.

Ignoring the "perpetual" principle of the Sabbath robs you of a wonderful opportunity to breathe—to be refreshed.

In observant Jewish households throughout the centuries, a particular ritual has marked the beginning of Shabbat. Shortly before the sun sinks below the horizon, two candles are lit. These two candles represent the two instances in the Torah in which God ordained the Sabbath. The first is in Exodus Chapter 20 where God commands the people to "remember" the Sabbath. The second is in Deuteronomy Chapter 5 where the command is to "observe" the Sabbath. There's a lesson for us there. It's important to *remember*. But it's even more important to *observe*.

For centuries, observing the Sabbath has meant a quiet, uncomplicated day of enjoying good food, talking, reading, walking, and napping. What's wrong with that? What is wrong with doing nothing one day a week? Nothing, of course! Especially since God commanded it. Yet for many of God's people today, spending a full day each week that way is unthinkable. It's scandalous. They would feel too guilty. They can't imagine not checking the phone for texts or emails every six to seven minutes. They can't comprehend not constantly monitoring social media to see who is eating what at which restaurant, or knowing what we're all supposed to be outraged or dismayed about this hour.

This slowness, quietness, and simplicity is a shock to the modern system. But it's a shock we all desperately need. Frankly, the lack of these things is killing us, which brings us to the third powerful reason for embracing the principle of the Sabbath.

3. There are consequences when we don't rest.

Remember the man who lost his life for gathering firewood on the Sabbath day? They found a man gathering sticks. Not murdering someone, mind you. Not sacrificing one of his kids to the demon Moloch. Gathering sticks. In Numbers 15 we discover: "And those who found him gathering sticks brought him to Moses and Aaron, and to all the congregation. They put him under guard..."[16]

Notice that the people made a citizen's arrest. They apprehended this maniac and "put him under guard." They stationed the best, well-armed tough guys right outside this guy's jail cell. Of course they did; he was a stick gatherer! Better lock this lunatic down, lest he break loose and gather some more sticks!

I'm joking, of course. But what happened to this man is no joke. They brought him to Moses. Moses inquired of the Lord. And the Lord decreed that the man should be put to death.[17] If this seems

---

16. vv. 33–34
17. See Exodus 15:35, 36

overly harsh to you, please allow me to remind you that the entire fate of humanity—the success of God's grand plan to undo the tragic consequences of Adam's rebellion, and the eternal destinies of every person who would one day be able to call upon the name of the Lord and be saved—hinged upon the success of the Israelite nation to survive through fifteen more centuries. If the tribes of Israel died out before the fullness of time, there would be no tribe of Judah. And without a tribe of Judah, there would be no Jesus born in Bethlehem, a descendant of David on His mother's side.

The stakes could not possibly have been higher. Again, the commandments God gave the people of Israel were very much about keeping them intact, healthy, and successful as a people, so "...when the fullness of the time had come, God sent forth His Son, born of a woman, born under the law, to redeem those who were under the law, that we might receive the adoption as sons."[18]

> The commandments God gave the people of Israel were very much about keeping them intact, healthy, and successful as a people.

It's illuminating to note which commandments carried the death penalty under the law of Moses. Only four violations warranted the harshest possible punishment. Three of them were murder, adultery, and chronic rebellion in children. That's right parents, you can tell your recalcitrant teenager that he or she should be grateful we're living under the New Covenant! Compliance with each of these was absolutely vital to keeping Israelite society strong and healthy. You already know what the fourth capital crime was: profaning the Sabbath.

---

18. Galatians 4:4, 5

Clearly, honoring a weekly day of rest was a key and necessary element in God's plan to keep the Jewish people successful and thriving through the ages.

If there were extreme consequences for failing to observe the Sabbath under the Old Covenant, should it surprise us that there are negative consequences if we do so today? I'm not talking about divine punishment. I'm talking about experiencing the natural, negative impacts that God was graciously trying to keep His people from experiencing in the first place. The reason God created harsh penalties for profaning the Sabbath under the Old Covenant was that, as our Designer, He knew we weren't built to run seven days a week, week after week. We break down. We end up running on empty physical, emotional, mental, and spiritual tanks. That's simply not sustainable.

In a sense, a lifestyle of ignoring the principle of the Sabbath still carries the death penalty! It's slow suicide.

Unwrap the Gift

As bad as that is, there is still another negative consequence of neglecting the principle of the Sabbath. As we've already seen, we forfeit God's supernatural blessing. When we take a step of faith and trust, and unplug for a day each week, we activate heavenly provision and support. A faithful God responds to that faith by meeting us not only with supernatural joy and refreshment on that day, but also heavenly favor and Spirit-empowered productivity on the other six days.

> A faithful God responds to that faith by meeting us…[with] heavenly favor.

What a gift the principle of the Sabbath is! Yet the vast majority of God's people never unwrap it. Instead they trudge wearily through life in their own ever-diminishing strength and resources. They get done only what their own cleverness and striving can accomplish. They forfeit divine appointments, supernatural favor, and miraculous increase. The kicker is, the physical and mental resources they're counting on are constantly exhausted and worn thin. They're running on empty tanks.

Who in their right mind would knowingly choose that option? Who would rather spend seven days a week struggling wearily on their own than take one day a week off and enjoy the help of the mighty Creator of the universe, while feeling sharper, stronger, and healthier as you do? Yet most of God's people are choosing the first option, apparently because we think the fourth commandment is the only one that doesn't still contain wisdom for us today.

Yes, the Sabbath is a gift. It's life, not law. This is precisely what Jesus was communicating when He told the Pharisees, "The Sabbath was made for man, and not man for the Sabbath." Observant Jewish people through the millennia have understood this. There is an ancient Jewish saying that I love: "More than Israel has kept Shabbat, Shabbat has kept Israel."[19]

God is imploring you to give yourself the gift of rest one day each week. Trust God and treat yourself. You'll be astonished at how much more you accomplish and how much more you enjoy the journey.

---

19. Tracey R. Rich, "Judaism 101: Shabbat," Jewfaq.Org, accessed 25 June 2019, http://www.jewfaq.org/shabbat.htm.

CHAPTER SIX

THE GETAWAY

Taking sabbaticals was the best business idea and perhaps also the best creative idea I've ever had.

—Stefan Sagmeister (Globally
Renowned Artist/Designer)

Does God care more about dirt than He does about you? That's a serious question I'd like you to consider for a moment. Do you think that God has less regard for your well-being and health than He does for common dirt?

I ask because, as we've already seen, when God was creating the laws and covenant ordinances specifically designed to create a successful Israelite society, he put in place very specific rules about giving farm soil a whole year off every seventh year. That's right; by divine law, the dirt was to get a year-long vacation after six years of hard, productive work. In Leviticus Chapter 25 we find:

And the LORD spoke to Moses on Mount Sinai, saying, "Speak to the children of Israel, and say to them: 'When you come into the land which I give you, then the land shall keep a sabbath to the LORD. Six years you shall sow your field, and six years you shall prune your vineyard, and gather its fruit; but in the seventh year there shall be a sabbath of solemn rest for the land, a sabbath to the LORD. You shall neither sow your field nor prune your vineyard. What grows of its own accord of your harvest you shall not reap, nor gather the grapes of your untended vine, *for it is a year of rest for the land.*"[1] (emphasis added)

There it is, right there in black and white. God decreed "a year of rest for the land" every seventh year. As every farmer or agronomist will tell you, topsoil is a living thing. And all living things need rest. God cared enough about dirt to see that it got periodic rest so it could remain healthy and productive, decade after decade, century after century. In Hebrew, this Sabbath year for the land was called the *shmita.* And it didn't only extend to land. It also gave all the working farm animals a break as well. If you were a pair of oxen used for plowing or a donkey that carried heavy loads to and from the fields, you got a year off, too.

So again, I ask you: Does God care more about dirt and donkeys than He does about you? Of course not! As Jesus reminded His disciples once, to God you are far more valuable than the birds of the air or the flowers of the field.[2] God loves people. So much so, that He sacrificed His only Son so that you and I could be restored to relationship with Him and enjoy connection to Him forever and ever. Yes, God cares about animals and flowers. He's *that* good and *that* loving, but He cares infinitely more about us. The fact is, the Sabbath and *shmita* laws are both expressions of that goodness and love. He's not trying to make things harder for His people; He's trying to help us!

---

1. Leviticus 25:1–5
2. See Matthew 6:26–28

In fact, God makes this clear right in the middle of giving His chosen people the *shmita* commandment. He said, "So you shall observe My statutes and keep My judgments, and perform them; and you will dwell in the land in safety. *Then the land will yield its fruit, and you will eat your fill, and dwell there in safety.*"[3] (emphasis added). Obedience would result in blessing. Doing things God's way always produces good results. Notice that the result of obedience here would be both abundance and security. He tells His people they will both "eat their fill" and "dwell in safety."

> The result of obedience here would be both abundance and security.

At the same time, everything we do with God, in God, for God, and through God requires faith. God designed it that way from the very start. For Adam and Eve, leaving that one, forbidden tree alone was a test of faith and trust in God. As we know, it's a test they failed. As I've pointed out repeatedly, observing the Sabbath requires faith as well. So, we shouldn't be surprised that obeying the command to rest the land for a year every seventh year required trust in God, too. God recognized this, because He addressed the issue right after He gave the *shmita* instructions. Our heavenly Father anticipated their concerns and fears about not planting, cultivating, and harvesting for a whole year. Immediately after assuring them that they'd experience provision and protection *if* they obeyed, He went on to say:

> "And if you say, 'What shall we eat in the seventh year, since we shall not sow nor gather in our produce?' Then I will

---

3. Leviticus 25:18, 19

command My blessing on you in the sixth year, and it will bring forth produce enough for three years."[4]

God knew that the people of Israel would be concerned about how they would live if they completely stopped farming for an entire year. Doing no planting, cultivating, or harvesting for a full year had multiyear implications. Not only would they not have food during that *shmita* year, they would also be without food for much of the following year as well, because it takes time to plant, cultivate, and reap a harvest. God recognized this and made them an extraordinary promise. He assured them that in the sixth year of each cycle, He'd bless them with enough of a harvest to last three years—enough to meet their needs for year six, with enough left over to get them through the *shmita* year seven, and right through year one of the next cycle, until the new harvest could be brought in. A triple-abundance blessing!

However, all of these instructions and promises were merely hypothetical as long as the Israelite tribes were encamped in the wilderness on the east side of the Jordan River. Only after crossing the river and settling in the land of promise would their faithfulness to these commands be tested. Only then would God get an opportunity to respond to their trustful obedience by pouring out supernatural blessing.

To Shmita, or Not to Shmita, That Is the Question

Let's imagine, for a moment, two households among the hundreds of thousands of Israelite families that entered the land of promise

---

4. Leviticus 25:20, 21

with Joshua leading the way. Let's call them the Smith family and the Jones family. Let's also suppose our two imaginary families were from the tribe of Zebulun. When the twelve tribes drew lots to determine which part of Canaan each tribe would be conquering, Tribe Zebulun learned it would be putting down roots in the northern part of Canaan, in the area just west of the large lake that will one day be called the Sea of Galilee. The farmers among Tribe Zebulun must have been thrilled at this news. They had been assigned the greenest, most fertile, most well-watered section in all of Canaan. It truly was a land flowing with milk and honey. And so the Smiths and Joneses settled in the heart of what is now called the Beit Netofa Valley, the breadbasket of modern Israel. The flat floor of the valley is ideal for growing grains such as barley. And the surrounding hillsides are perfect for growing olives, almonds, figs, and grapes.

Both the Smiths and the Joneses established farms on large acreages in the area. Both families spent the first several years learning how to make the land productive, how the seasons unfolded in this new land, and what was best to plant in each particular part of the year. At the end of their sixth year in the land, both the Smiths and the Joneses experienced the greatest harvest season yet. It seemed that every tree, vine, and stalk on the property was so loaded with fruit that it might collapse under the weight. Their barns literally overflowed with plenty.

At this point, the stories of the Smiths and Joneses take different paths. As the sixth year in the land came to a close and their seventh year approached, both were faced with a significant decision—whether or not to obey God's instructions to give the land a Sabbath year of rest.

The head of the Smith clan viewed the spectacular harvest of year six as primarily the product of his hard work and clever farming ability. This level of abundance, he assumed, was their "new normal." He thought, "I've got this farming thing figured out! If I did it this year, I can do it every year." The bumper crop not only gave him enough for his family for the year, but plenty leftover to sell in the markets of the other eleven tribes. In other words, Mr. Smith saw a golden opportunity to increase his wealth. Of course, selling the surplus meant he would need to plant again the next year—year seven. And why wouldn't he? He was clearly a master farmer! He was making it look easy.

Mr. Jones, on the other hand, saw the amazing abundance of year six for what it really was—the supernatural fulfillment of God's promise to provide three years' worth of provision in a single year. With that in view, he stored and preserved his overflow, knowing that he was about to allow the land to enjoy its well-earned *shmita* rest the following year. That year of rest for the land was also a break for the Jones family. There was much less to do and so they were able to refresh, recuperate, and grow closer together. As the grapes, figs, almonds, and other fruits ripened, he invited the poor of the area to come and help themselves to whatever they could pick and carry. This, too, God had instructed in giving his command

> They were able to refresh, recuperate, and grow closer together.

concerning the *shmita*, but it still felt good to help people who were struggling. And by being gracious to the poor, Mr. Jones further invited God's blessings upon him and his family. The rest of the produce that year simply fell to the ground, enriching and fertilizing the soil. Animals grazed freely on the fields, further fertilizing the earth.

A year later, Mr. Smith was disappointed to learn that the abundance of year six wasn't his new normal after all. His lands produced far less than they did in year seven. He needed every bit of what he harvested, so there was nothing left for the poor. In contrast, Mr. Jones's fields, orchards, and vineyards yielded abundantly after their year of rest.

Fast-forward fifty years into the future: the sons and grandsons of Smith and Jones are now operating their respective farms. But the Smith farm's soils are depleted—exhausted of all nutrients and minerals. Their yields have been diminishing for decades. Meanwhile, they've watched the Jones clan continue to bring in bumper crops year after year. And they've watched them repeatedly let perfectly good fruits, nuts, grains, and vegetables rot on the vine every seventh year.

Two families. Two different choices. Two different outcomes. In essence, the choice was greed or grace. Mr. Smith chose greed. He forgot the very thing that Moses had implored them to remember once they entered the land of promise:

Beware that you do not forget the LORD your God by not keeping His commandments, His judgments, and His statutes which I command you today, lest—when you have eaten and are full, and have built beautiful houses and dwell in them; and when your herds and your flocks multiply, and your silver and your gold are multiplied, and all that you have is multiplied; when your heart is lifted up, and you forget the LORD your God who brought you out of the land of Egypt, from the house of bondage; who led you through that great and terrible wilderness, in which were fiery serpents and scorpions and thirsty land where there was no water; who brought water for you out of the flinty rock; who fed you in the wilderness with manna, which your fathers did not know, that He might humble you and that He might test you, to do you good in the end—then you say in your heart, 'My power and the might of my hand have gained me this wealth.' And you shall remember the LORD your God, for it is He who gives you power to get wealth, that He may establish His covenant which He swore to your fathers, as it is this day."[5]

Mr. Jones chose grace. He chose to trust in God's goodness and faithfulness. As a result, he experienced abundant favor, manifested in supernatural blessing, sustained abundance, and good health.

We've already seen that the principle of the Sabbath still contains wisdom for you and me today. Not in a legalistic way, but in a way that imparts life and blessing. So, is there also a principle for us modern folks to apply embedded in the Old Covenant law of *shmita*? Even if we're not farmers? I believe so. Let's explore that question.

> The principle of the Sabbath still contains wisdom for you and me today.

The Power of a Sabbatical

Without a doubt, resting one day out of seven is a powerful and important thing. But there is another step to take if we want to incorporate all of God's wisdom concerning rest. You see, God gave Israel both the Sabbath *and* the *shmita*. There is a place for both in our lives today.

---

5. Deuteronomy 8:11–18

The ancient biblical practice of letting the land rest every seventh year has an echo that has been in place in our culture for a long time. Perhaps you've heard a friend or acquaintance—maybe someone in the field of academics—talk about taking a sabbatical.

No doubt you noticed that the word looks very much like the word Sabbath, and for good reason. The English word "sabbatical" is rooted in the Hebrew word *shabbat*, and somewhere along the way was transliterated into the Latin word *sabbaticus* and the Greek word *sabbatikos*—all of which generally refer to taking an extended rest. That's right, our current concept of a sabbatical is rooted in the biblical practice of *shmita*.

Few people today can afford to take a full year off. At least they assume they can't. Business owners and self-employed contractors are especially likely to assume that even the thought of taking a full year off every seventh year is total insanity.

That's certainly what Stefan Sagmeister thought, until he just hauled off and tried it. Back in the 1990s, Sagmeister, a gifted artist and designer, found himself operating one of New York City's hottest design houses. He was well-known both as a modern artist and for designing album covers and concert posters for some of the biggest names in music. Increasingly in demand, he churned out a remarkable amount of work year after year. But by 1999 he felt himself getting creatively stale. He began to feel that he was repackaging the same ideas in different forms rather than coming up with truly innovative concepts. So, in 2001, he did something unthinkable for most self-employed people. After scrimping and socking away money for a few months, he shut his company down for an entire year. He just locked up and headed for southeast Asia to wander around for a year.

Sagmeister talks about that decision in a popular 2009 TED

Talk titled, "The Power of Time Off." In it he admits to wondering at the time if he was making a catastrophic business decision. He wondered if all his regular clients would find someone else while he was off. He wondered if the design world would forget about him and move on. He feared he might lose all the progress and forward momentum he had worked so hard for years to build. Yet he feared something else even more. He feared continuing to do work he didn't feel proud of. So, he let his clients and associates know he was shutting the business down for a year, and off he went.

What Sagmeister experienced sounds almost miraculous. The change of scenery and the rest revitalized him. He carried a sketch pad and pen with him constantly and found himself harvesting ideas everywhere. The experience was transformative. When he returned to his business, he was filled with both creativity and passion for his craft. All of his clients came flocking back, and he produced better work than ever before. In fact, shortly after coming back he won a Grammy for his design of a box set of music by Talking Heads, and won a National Design Award that same year. Near the end of his TED Talk, Sagmeister lists the positive effects of his first sabbatical:

- My job became my calling again
- It was very enjoyable
- Over the long term it was financially successful
- Everything we designed in the seven years following that first sabbatical had originated in that year[6]

6. Stefan Sagmeister, "The Power of Time Off," Ted.Com, 2009, https://www.ted.com/talks/stefan_sagmeister_the_power_of_time_off.

Sagmeister is, to my knowledge, neither Jewish nor Christian. Yet by daring to take a yearlong sabbatical, he intuitively activated an ancient wisdom principle in God's Word—the principle of the *shmita*. It is a practice he continues to this day. Every seventh year, he shuts everything down and takes up residence in some new corner of the world to rest, recharge, and renew. In 2014, he told an interviewer, "Taking sabbaticals was the best business idea and perhaps also the best creative idea I've ever had."[7] The fact is, God's wisdom principles will work for anyone, even people who don't believe in Him. But what unbelievers miss out on is the additional element of God's supernatural power and provision.

> God's wisdom principles will work for anyone, even people who don't believe in Him.

I can hear you thinking now, "Are you serious, Morris? I was still trying to get my mind around completely unplugging for one full day each week, and now you're telling me I need to take a whole year off every seventh year!?"

Actually, no. You will be relieved to learn that's *not* what I'm telling you. (Although if you could do so, I have no doubt it would yield even bigger dividends than what Stefan Sagmeister experienced because of God's supernatural power and blessing.)

Clearly, very few of us can take an entire year off. Those of us with family obligations, employees, or employers—and that's most of us—simply can't shut everything down for a year at a time. So how *can* you and I incorporate sabbaticals into our lives here in the twenty-first century? Here's good news: it's possible!

---

7. Alex Soojung-Kim Pang, *Rest: Why You Get More Done When You Work Less* (New York: Basic Books, 2016), 224.

More Than a Vacation

Let's begin by reminding ourselves that we're applying a principle here, not a law. The *shmita* principle is that periodic extended breaks from being "productive" can have a powerful restorative effect on body, soul, and spirit—just as a season of rest can restore the soil of a farm. You'll recall that when my years of ignoring the principle of the Sabbath finally caught up with me, an eight-week sabbatical was able to set me right.

After my restorative sabbatical, we instituted a sabbatical policy for pastoral staff at Gateway Church. Every seven years, our pastors are given a paid six-week sabbatical in which they are strongly urged to completely unplug from ministry and do whatever refreshes and recharges them. Again, I know not everyone can manage an unbroken six-week stretch away from work. But even an extra week or two of extended, unplugged rest every few years can work wonders.

Please understand, I'm not talking about simply taking a vacation. Frankly, the way many people do vacations, they end up more exhausted than if they'd kept working. How many times have you heard someone say, "I need a vacation to recover from my vacation!"? Perhaps you've said that yourself.

As we're about to discover, a sabbatical is both more and less than a vacation. Yet a vacation—even a tiring one—is at least a change of scenery. Many of us aren't even taking vacations anymore. In rising numbers and to an increasing degree, Americans are so driven and desperate to succeed, we're leaving paid vacation days unused. It's true.

A study conducted by the U.S. Travel Association for an initiative called Project: Time Off calculated that businesses and other organizations in the United States were holding a total of $224 billion in unused paid time off. And that as the calendar flipped over from 2014 to 2015, employees carried over $65.6 billion of accrued, unused vacation time.[8] That study revealed even more shocking statistics:

> From 2000 to 2013, the average employee has steadily reduced the amount of vacation time taken, from 20.9 days per year to just 16 (in other countries, up to 41 days off are granted each year). As a result, many employees end up with a considerable amount of accrued unused vacation. The situation is worst in midsized firms with 100 to 499 employees, where the figure per employee is 7.6 days.[9]

At first blush, this trend—employees who don't take paid time away—may seem like a win for the businesses that employ them. But it's not. Increasingly businesses are realizing that having a burned-out, stressed-out, weary, mentally fuzzy, emotionally fragile workforce isn't exactly a great thing for productivity and efficiency. For example, a special report by the U.S. Travel Association titled, "Under-Vacationed America: A State-by-State Look at Time Off" found that workers who use the majority of their vacation days for travel are significantly happier than those who travel less or not at all. Americans taking all or most of their vacation days to travel report being 20 percent happier with their personal relationships

---

8. Fran Howarth, "The Perils of Unused Vacation Time," Spark, 2018, https://www.adp.com/spark/articles/2018/07/the-perils-of-unused-vacation-time.aspx.

9. Howarth, "Unused Vacation Time."

and 56 percent happier with their health and well-being than those who travel with little or none of their vacation time.[10]

How out of balance are we as a culture when many of us won't stay home even when they'll pay us to do it? Even if we do take a break from the workplace for a week or so, most of us still feel compelled to constantly check email and monitor developments, if for no other reason than to avoid being hopelessly behind when we return! But again, vacations aren't the answer. We need both Sabbaths (*shabbats*) and sabbaticals (*shmitas*). And a sabbatical is more than a vacation. It's really a series of Sabbath days strung together. A sabbatical is an extended period of quiet, stillness, rest, reflection, prayer, and fellowship with God and His Word. It's a string of days in which we do pretty much nothing, and do it with both intentionality and expectancy.

> A sabbatical is an extended period of quiet, stillness, rest, reflection, prayer, and fellowship.

The Modified Sabbatical

Back in the 1980s, when Microsoft was just beginning to emerge as a global tech giant, company founder, CEO, and chairman Bill Gates discovered the power of going away and being alone for a week in a remote place once a year. Gates annually retreated to a tiny cabin on a largely uninhabited island off the coast of Washington state accessible only by seaplane. These weeks became vital

10. "Under-Vacationed America: A State-By-State Look At Time Off," U.S. Travel Association, 2018, https://www.ustravel.org/research/under-vacationed-america-state-state-look-time.

times to step away from the constant cyclone of meetings, decisions, and day-to-day details and look at the bigger picture. It was a time to think deeply and read widely. He and his executive staff started calling these annual getaways his "think week." One author noted:

> During one famous think week in 1995, Gates realized the importance of the Internet to Microsoft's future business; he returned from other think weeks determined to move Microsoft into Web browsers, tablets, and online gaming. As a result, Gate's think week has since been imitated by executives at Microsoft and a number of Silicon Valley companies.[11]

Again, Bill Gates and others have stumbled onto a spiritual principle that works. But sabbaticals are so much more powerful when you add the element of the Spirit of God to the equation. That's exactly what one of the most successful Christian businessmen I've ever known started doing years ago. In fact, he'll tell you his regular sabbaticals are a major reason he was so wildly successful in business.

I'm talking about Steve Dulin, who also happens to be a good friend and one of the founding elders of Gateway Church. Steve founded a commercial construction company and saw it grow at an amazing rate across two decades. His company was extremely successful by any standard of measurement. As it grew, he began to accept invitations to speak to groups of Christian entrepreneurs and business owners about how to grow their businesses God's way. This eventually grew into a full-fledged ministry. That ministry's

---

11. Alex Soojung-Kim Pang, *Rest: Why You Get More Done When You Work Less* (New York: Basic Books, 2016), 225–226.

mission is "...to train leaders and businesspeople to effectively apply proven biblical principles to every area of their lives and businesses so they may achieve the greatest measures of success and impact the world for Christ."[12]

A few years ago, he sensed God telling him to sell his business, and move into ministry full time. Now, I shared stewardship-related stories about Steve and his wife, Melody, in both *The Blessed Life* and *Beyond Blessed*. What I've never shared is that one of his most powerful secrets to making wise business decisions is the sabbatical. Steve is a passionate and persuasive advocate of taking regular, weeklong stretches, alone, away from the demands and distractions of daily work life. What he advocates is not unlike Bill Gates's "think weeks," but with the infinitely more powerful spiritual factor of God's presence involved.

Steve's testimony is that once he discovered the power of a sabbatical, he began planning at least one and sometimes several of them on his annual calendar. He began to view these times as the most important thing he did for both his business and his family. He would book a cabin in a remote, isolated area with room to walk. He didn't want to see or hear another human being. The only voices he wanted to hear for an entire week were his own and God's. No television. No telephones. No technology.

> The only voices he wanted to hear for an entire week were his own and God's.

Steve will tell you that his best ideas, his clearest vision, his most vital discernment, and his wisest decisions invariably came out of

---

12. "History, Mission, & Vision," Masterplan Business Ministries, accessed 25 June 2019, https://www.masterplanministries.org/history-mission-vision.

these sabbatical seasons with God. Now Steve freely shares his secret with others. Provided here with his permission are his eighteen keys to experiencing a successful sabbatical:

1. Start preparing for the sabbatical about a week ahead of time. Begin to consciously slow down your mind and thoughts so that you will be prepared to focus on the Lord rather than work, projects, issues, etc.

2. Bring plenty of paper, pens, pencils, and/or highlighters.

3. Try to do some type of fast during the sabbatical. Fasting makes your spirit more sensitive to the Lord. If possible, start fasting the day before your sabbatical as part of your preparation.

4. Bring warm clothes. Fasting tends to make you feel colder than usual.

5. Drink plenty of pure water to flush out any toxins brought out by the fast.

6. As you start your sabbatical, pray over your room and dedicate the sabbatical to the Lord. Ask the Lord to come and ask the Holy Spirit to fill the room.

7. Try to keep your focus on the Lord. I avoid all newspapers, magazines, and television. It is fine to bring a few books along, but it is usually best to keep them to a minimum. It is easy to get involved in reading a book and "lose" a lot of time.

8. Use this time to build your relationship with God. It can be beneficial to read books written by people who are further along in their relationship with the Lord than we are, so we can learn from them how to get closer to the Lord. Once again, I keep this to a minimum.

9. Do not go into the sabbatical with a set agenda. Pray that God's agenda will be accomplished. The purpose is not to get something from God, but to spend time with Him.

10. This is typically not the best time to do an in-depth Bible study on a specific topic. It can be very time consuming and distract you from spending time with God and hearing from Him.

11. Keep outside contact to a minimum. I check in with my family once every two or three days and avoid outside conversations.

12. It is good to get out of your room periodically. I like to take a quiet walk once a day and sometimes walk at night. There is nothing wrong with doing an activity that takes your mind off the sabbatical as long as it is for a short time.

13. Create a blank to-do list at the beginning of the sabbatical. Anytime you think of a task that you need to do at work, at home, etc., immediately write it on this list so you don't have to spend time thinking about or trying to remember it.

14. Ask the Lord if there are specific areas that He wants you to focus on during the sabbatical. I usually begin the sabbatical by asking the Lord to reveal to me any sin in my life that I am not aware of.

15. Bring or create a prayer list with specific needs in your life and in the lives of others so you can pray about them. I leave space to write down anything the Lord speaks to me about people and their needs.

16. For organizational purposes, I usually list on separate pieces of paper any topics in my life that I feel the Lord may want to address (ex. ministry, relationships, family, to-do, work, etc.). I place these pages into different areas of a binder so

that each topic is easy to find when I need to write down things the Lord is saying. I also have a general topic entitled "Sabbatical (Year)" where I can write anything the Lord says that is not under a specific topic.

17. Ask the Lord what He wants to do in the coming year and then use the results from your sabbatical as a guide to keep you on course until your next sabbatical.

18. Do not strive to hear the Lord. Submit your will to His will and ask Him to speak to you and direct and guide you. Ask Him to give you revelation as you read the Word. The Lord wants to speak to you more than you want to hear from Him.

A Sabbatical for Your Most Important Relationship

Another key member of Gateway's leadership team has long championed a special variation of the classic sabbatical. One of our founding elders, the founder of the global marriage enrichment ministry MarriageToday, Jimmy Evans, recommends that married couples take a sabbatical together periodically to do much of the same kind of thing.

Jimmy knows and teaches that couples have much stronger relationships and build healthier, more successful families when they have a shared vision and hear from God together. And the best way to do that is to periodically take what he calls a "vision retreat"— a sabbatical for couples. Jimmy has written, "After many years of investing time in an annual vision retreat, Karen and I can tell you it is one of the most powerful and productive things you can do for your marriage and family."[13] MarriageToday produced a guide to help couples prepare for and get the most out of a vision retreat. It encourages couples to consider including many or all of the following elements into a retreat:

- Prayer (Pray with each other and for each other.)
- Bible Study (Use a devotional or go through a study together.)
- Journaling (Write down what you hear God speaking to you as a couple.)
- Fun (Do things you both enjoy together.)
- Romance (Be intentional and thoughtful about stoking the fire of passion in your relationship.)
- Communication (Talk! Even if it's not your nature or temperament to do so!)[14]

If you're married, imagine what disconnecting from the busyness and pressures of daily life and getting alone with your spouse in a quiet place for several days might do for your relationship. This very special variety of sabbatical carries the power to revitalize your relationship and, more importantly, give you both an opportunity to hear from God together. Just as you require recharging and renewing

> Just as you require recharging and renewing as an individual from time to time, so does your most important relationship.

---

13. Jimmy Evans and Karen Evans, *The Mountaintop of Marriage: A Vision Retreat Guidebook* (MarriageToday, 2008), 4.

14. Evans, *Mountaintop of Marriage*, 4.

as an individual from time to time, so does your most important relationship.

In the course of your couples sabbatical, God will very likely speak direction and vision for your family to you. He'll give you divine goals and heavenly strategies for achieving them. You'll receive both insights and goals about your finances, your children, work lives, and much more. You're likely to find yourselves getting on the same page in ways you didn't know were possible.

A sabbatical, whether as a couple or alone, is a powerful thing—especially when you add God to the mix.

Unleashing Supernatural Creativity

Jesus only had a three-year ministry. As the Gospels reveal, it was surely one of the busiest, most intense three years any human has ever experienced. He ping-ponged back and forth across the land of Israel, preaching, teaching, and healing in every village and synagogue in the land.[15] Not only was Jesus constantly in demand and surrounded by crowds, but the invisible spiritual warfare surrounding Him must have been beyond our ability to imagine. It's no exaggeration to say that no human being in history ever had a more demanding and draining three-year run than did Jesus of Nazareth.

That's why it's interesting to note that Jesus launched his ministry with an extended sabbatical. After His baptism He was compelled by the Spirit of God to head out alone into the deserts south and east of Judah. We also know that Jesus' forty-day sabbatical

---

15. Matthew 9:35: "Then Jesus went about all the cities and villages, teaching in their synagogues, preaching the gospel of the kingdom, and healing every sickness and every disease among the people."

TAKE THE DAY OFF

involved an extreme form of fasting. That makes sense because Jesus was preparing Himself for the most extreme mission in all of history—the redemption of an entire planet.

Yet even after that initial sabbatical, the Gospels show us Jesus slipping away as frequently as possible for time alone with God. It seems the greater the demands and pressures upon Him grew, the more deliberate Jesus became about finding ways to get alone with God. There is a huge and vital lesson in this for us.

If Jesus Himself found it necessary to unplug, disconnect, and find some quiet space with God, how much more important is it that we do so? Read the Gospels through this lens and you'll find that nearly every time Jesus withdrew for a season, He returned with fresh direction, insight, or knowledge of what was about to take place.

Contrast that to the way we live today. The fact is, most of us have grown so accustomed to walking around with our mental tanks nearly empty, that we think that's normal for us. We call it "brain fog." Or we blame our forgetfulness and inability to focus on getting older. We sense we're not as creative and innovative as we used to be, but that, too, we blame on aging, or simply being "too busy."

The fact is, God designed us to be creative. The ability to be creative is one of the key ways that we're made "in the image and likeness of God." He's a Creator, and you've been made in His image. One of the great tragedies of the modern, unrested lifestyle is that it eventually robs us of this most extraordinary of divine gifts. That's what makes a sabbatical so powerful and so very important. Among its many blessings and benefits, it restores and replenishes your creativity.

> God designed us to be creative.

Have you ever been trying to remember something—a name, a song title, or an actor's name—and just couldn't come up with it? Then a few minutes later, when you'd given up, the item popped suddenly into your head? Something similar often happens when facing a seemingly unsolvable problem. You think and think, stew and strive and strain, yet can see no possible solution. Then you wake up the next morning and you know exactly what to do. The answer is as obvious as a blinking neon sign. If just a tiny sliver of quiet, disengagement, or rest can give you little breakthroughs like that, imagine what an extended period with those things could do for your mind.

Now, be honest: When I described the ideal sabbatical above and shared Steve Dulin's guidelines for carrying out a sabbatical, the following thought crossed your mind, didn't it? *Um... that sounds really boring!*

I understand the thought. But actually, that's a part of what makes a sabbatical so powerful. We're overstimulated. Our brains have learned to expect a constant stream of input—often from multiple directions at once. In fact, we can easily become addicted to the constant bombardment. This makes us uncomfortable with silence. Quiet... bothers us. But even the secular, scientific world is beginning to understand that we have been designed to need regular, extended seasons of quiet, stillness, and even boredom, if we're going to function at our highest. That's right, boredom!

In a July 2017 article in the online technology magazine *Quartz*, writer Jordan Rosenfeld authored a piece carrying the headline, "I kicked my smartphone addiction by retraining my brain to enjoy being bored."[16] In it, she shared how the advent of the smartphone,

---

16. Jordan Rosenfeld, "I Kicked My Smartphone Addiction By Retraining My Brain To Enjoy Being Bored," *Quartz*, 2017, https://qz.com/1020976/the-scientific-link-between-boredom-and-creativity/.

and her growing dependence on it, steadily drained all the quiet, reflective, "boring" moments out of her days:

Before long, I was never bored: not at the post office, the grocery store, or while getting my oil changed. None of this seemed like a problem—until I noticed a creeping feeling of mental clutter, and a significant decline in my creative writing. It hit me while I was driving one day: I no longer let myself be bored. I wondered just how bad that was for a writer—or for any other creative type. And so I decided to dive into the research on the unexpected benefits of boredom.

What Rosenfeld discovered was lots of research revealing a link between periods of stillness and inactivity (aka "boredom"), and creative breakthroughs. We clearly need mental quiet and stillness—an unstimulated state we might describe as being bored—in order to function at our highest mentally. And this is just what Sabbaths and sabbaticals provide. Stefan Sagmeister says, "Everyone whose job description includes 'thinking' or coming up with ideas will benefit [from taking a sabbatical]."[17]

Again, this doesn't even take into consideration the God factor. How much more beneficial a sabbatical is when you not only allow your body and soul to rest deeply, but also invite the Spirit of God to fill you and speak to you. Nothing is more refreshing than communion

> Nothing is more refreshing than communion with God.

---

17. Stefan Sagmeister, "The Power of Time Off," Ted.Com, 2009, https://www.ted.com/talks/stefan_sagmeister_ the_power_of_time_off.

with God. It is literally like eating from the tree of life. With that in mind, read the opening lines of the 23rd psalm with fresh eyes. Here's how The Passion Translation renders those familiar verses:

The Lord is my best friend and my shepherd.
I always have more than enough.
He offers a resting place for me in his luxurious love.
His tracks take me to an oasis of peace, the quiet brook of bliss.
That's where he restores and revives my life.
He opens before me pathways to God's pleasure
and leads me along in his footsteps of righteousness
so that I can bring honor to his name.[18]

That is what extended time alone with God will do for you. In Jeremiah, right before announcing the New Covenant that will one day be inaugurated through Jesus, God says, "I will refresh the weary and satisfy the faint."[19]

That's our Father. That's what His presence does.

---

18. Psalm 23:1–3 TPT
19. Jeremiah 31:25 NIV

CHAPTER SEVEN

TOP PRIORITY

"The key is not to prioritize what's on your schedule but to schedule your priorities."

—Stephen Covey

In my part of the world, people take the Dallas Cowboys seriously. Very, very seriously. Yes, I know that's true of sports fans everywhere, but some of my fellow Texans' obsession with the Cowboys frequently flirts with crossing the line into outright idolatry.

To illustrate that truth, a story is told of a man who attended the Cowboys' sold out season opener one year and was surprised to see an empty seat beside a woman in front of him. She was dressed head to toe in Cowboys' silver, white, and blue regalia. During a time-out, the man asked the woman about the empty seat. "It was my husband's," she explained, "but he passed away. We never missed a home game." "I'm so sorry to hear that," the man replied. "But couldn't you find a relative who wanted to come to the game with you?" "No," she shrugged. "They all insisted on going to the funeral."

We all have our priorities. We tend to spend our time, just as with our money, in accordance with what we value most. Back when people wrote checks, I used to say, "Show me your checkbook register and I'll show you what you truly value." The same is true of your calendar. The problem is, we don't always value the right things.

You'll recall Stephen Covey's illustration about the "big rocks." We learned that if you don't put the big rocks in first, you'll never fit them in at all. The takeaway for us here is, if you want to make a Sabbath rest a regular part of your life—and hopefully by now you understand that you should—you're going to have to make it a priority. The question is, how? You're juggling multiple roles—spouse, parent, son or daughter, breadwinner, friend, church member, volunteer, and possibly several others—each of which is clamoring for attention and bombarding you with demands. If you're waiting until your schedule magically creates some time for rest for you, it will simply never happen. How can you make sure that the "big rock" of rest gets prioritized in the midst of all these other rocks, big and small, that want to go into your jar?

In my book, *Beyond Blessed*, which dealt mainly with biblical stewardship of finances, I pointed readers to a special tool for becoming a better steward of money—a budget. I wrote:

> A budget is simply a detailed plan that reflects your values and goals. Most households simply don't have a plan for getting to where they want to go. Think of a good budget as a map for arriving at your goals.[1]

When it comes to becoming a better steward of your time, you have a very similar tool at your disposal if you'll choose to use it.

---

1. Robert Morris, *Beyond Blessed: God's Perfect Plan To Overcome All Financial Stress* (New York: FaithWords, 2019), 206.

It's called a schedule. In his classic book, *The 7 Habits of Highly Effective People*, Stephen Covey famously wrote, "The key is not to prioritize what's on your schedule but to schedule your priorities." In other words, the most important goals you want to accomplish cannot live solely in your mind and heart. They're not truly *real* unless they're also on your calendar.

Scheduling priorities means more than putting them on a to-do list. Such lists, by their very nature, don't have deadlines. They're not appointments on your schedule or calendar with designated time allocated to them. No, you check off items on your to-do list when you get around to accomplishing them. Such a list can be helpful in determining your priorities based on your values. But a list can never allocate *time*.

Your calendar is your budget for stewarding your time. Most of us tend to think of our calendars as things where only appointments and meetings are noted. Most of these revolve around our 8:00 a.m. to 6:00 p.m. workdays. But the reality is that the world will rush in to fill all the blank spaces.

I once heard a pastor friend of mine ask a large gathering of fellow pastors, "How would you spend your time if God were in charge of your calendar?" He went on to point out that our calendars are our primary tool for helping us become *who* we want to become. He used the following example: If one year from now you want to be a better parent, can you show me where that lives on your calendar? Show me where

> If it isn't scheduled, it isn't a real goal.

intentional, focused time with your kids is blocked out in advance and protected as if it were a key business meeting. If it isn't scheduled, it isn't a real goal. It's nothing more than a good intention. A wish.

In other words, as my friend wisely reminded us, your calendar or schedule should be a detailed and accurate reflection of *who you want to become*, rather than just filled with *stuff you want to get done*. There's something powerful and activating about having a thing on your schedule. It moves it from the realm of the hypothetical to the realm of the real. Things on your calendar become real.

I have a friend who is a prolific and successful writer. Many people who aspire to be writers come to him for advice on how to get started. Hardly a week goes by that he doesn't hear from someone who knows they "have a book in them" but can't figure out how to get it out onto paper. It's obvious that they're looking for some sort of exotic, mysterious secret or trick that only writers know. His advice is always underwhelmingly simple. He tells them, "Writers write. So, start scheduling writing time into your day. And when that scheduled time arrives, plant your hindquarters in a chair in front of a keyboard and start stringing words together into sentences." That's just another way of saying, make your schedule reflect who you want to become and what you want to accomplish. This is precisely what one of the world's most successful novelists did to get started. Back when John Grisham was a practicing lawyer with an itch to write fiction, he took out his leather-bound day planner and wrote the single word "Write!" into sections of his calendar. The moment he did so, writing moved from being a *wish* to being an *appointment*. Time had been allocated.

This is no less true when it comes to rest. If you want to be a rested person—a person who recognizes and honors the wisdom of the principle of the Sabbath—then you're going to have to have a standing appointment with "rest." I've already described my encounter decades ago with a pastor friend who had clearly learned the power of this secret. You'll recall my effort to schedule a lunch meeting with him and my discovery that his calendar had the word "Nothing" written across the entire day of Thursday. Although I didn't understand it at the time, I now know that my friend had an important appointment on that Thursday—one he valued enough to protect, even at the risk of offending an acquaintance (me). You and I need to know how to do that as well. Let's talk about that.

Making Tough Choices

Some Christian books are evergreen. They continue to sell year after year, decade after decade. These marathon runners never go out of print because the needs they address are always present. By the grace of God, my first book, *The Blessed Life*, has become one of those. Another such book is the classic by Dr. Henry Cloud and Dr. John Townsend, *Boundaries: When to Say Yes, How to Say No to Take Control of Your Life*. There is a reason every Christian bookseller on earth keeps it on their shelves year after year. Clearly, a lot of us need help in learning to say no.

The moment you make the decision to make a Sabbath rest a priority and plant that flag on your schedule, I can promise, you'll immediately get a steady stream of opportunities to compromise that decision. Every one of those requests will be sincere, legitimate, and worthwhile. The fact is, in any given hour of any given day, there are thousands of "good" things you could be doing. Yet you can only do one thing at a time. You cannot do all the things. We have to *choose*. And you *will* choose. The

> In any given hour of any given day, there are thousands of "good" things you could be doing.

only remaining question is, "What will drive your choice?" Will it be emotion? Guilt? The pressure of others' expectations? Fear of rejection? False urgency? Insecurity? Or will something higher and eternal inform your decision? In *First Things First*, Stephen Covey calls this maintaining "integrity in the moment of choice."[2] About our God-given power of choice, he writes:

> We may find it convenient to live with the illusion that circumstances or other people are responsible for the quality of our lives, but the reality is that we are responsible—response-able— for our choices. And while some of these choices may seem small and insignificant at the time, like tiny mountain rivulets that come together to create a mighty river, these decisions join together to move us with increasing force toward our final destiny. Over time, our choices become habits of the heart. And, more than any other factor, these habits of the heart affect our time and the quality of our lives.[3]

Once you've made the decision to incorporate God's wisdom concerning rest into your weekly life, you're going to have to learn to defend and protect that decision. It wasn't always this way, but eventually I decided that certain things are nonnegotiable for me: God, my family, my work, and my health. Those are my values, my priorities. So, I now deliberately and intentionally schedule time to cultivate each of these nonnegotiables.

This isn't just a mental commitment to investing time in these

2. Stephen R. Covey, A. Roger Merrill and Rebecca R. Merrill, *First Things First* (New York: Free Press, 1994), 169.

3. Covey, *First Things First*, 169–170.

areas. They're not on a running, invisible to-do list I carry around in my head. No, I budget specific blocks of time for the things God has told me are most important for me and my calling. As a result, my wife doesn't have to settle for the scraps and leftovers of my time after I've met everyone else's demands and needs. She doesn't have to be content with the crumbs off the table of my time allocation. My calendar will testify of her importance to me, and her importance to God.

In other words, I formally, consistently schedule what is important, rather than leave things to chance and to my good intentions. I schedule time for work. I schedule time for family. I schedule time for rest. With time, just as with money, planning is vital. If you don't create a plan, our fallen, broken world will create one for you. It will fill your days with things that have no eternal impact, no connection to your goals, and have nothing to do with your highest values.

I keep referring to *Beyond Blessed*, my book about stewardship of finances, because money and time are so similar in many regards. And every Christian must be a wise steward of both to be an effective ambassador of God's kingdom. In that book I shared a valuable concept to help individuals and families make difficult decisions about finances. I described how Debbie and I had learned to yield our difficult financial decisions to the authority of "Mr. Budget."

In our early married years, I made very little money, and what I did earn came in sporadically and unevenly. We both knew that if we were going to achieve our goals of tithing, giving, and avoiding debt, we were going to have to live within a budget. So we made Mr. Budget an honorary member of our household. Mr. Budget was stern but wise. Whenever Debbie or I would be tempted to make an impulse purchase, the other learned to say, "Wow, that would be a cool thing to buy. Let's consult Mr. Budget!" And if the funds for such a purchase weren't allocated and available, the other of us would then say, "Hmm, Mr. Budget said no. What a wet blanket he is!" This kept either of us from having to be the bad guy in the eyes of the person we love. Mr. Budget is also a powerful ally in saying no to requests and invitations from others that involve spending money. A budget isn't subjective. It isn't a feeling.

Well, Mr. Budget has an ally in the daily battle to stay true to your goals and values: "Mr. Schedule." That is basically what my friend was doing all those years ago when I was trying to talk him into having lunch with me on his Sabbath. He was saying, "Robert, I'd love to get some time with you, but next Thursday is out. I asked 'Mr. Schedule' and he said I'm booked all that day. Booked doing 'nothing!'"

Putting First Things First

Once you begin the process of transferring your priorities, values, and goals from your heart to your calendar, you're going to be presented with a set of difficult choices. After all, there are only twenty-four hours in a day, only seven days in a week. And we need to spend roughly a third of that available time sleeping in order to be healthy and sustainably productive.

In other words, saying yes to the things that are most important will almost certainly require saying no to several, perhaps many, worthwhile things. This is a potentially painful but very healthy, vitally important process. For a person who has been spending more money than he or she takes in, going on a budget will require taking a hard, objective, nonemotional look at all the ways money has been spent and identifying expenses that can be reduced or eliminated altogether. In the same way, beginning to order your life in accordance with a schedule that reflects your highest values—especially the value of Sabbath rest—will require an equally ruthless look at the ways you spend time.

One of the most powerful ways to increase your available reserves of both time and money is to *simplify*. Most of us are living lives that are far more complicated than they need to be. We're simply trying to do too many things, be in too many places, and juggle too many responsibilities that, if we're honest with ourselves and God, lie outside our primary calling and goals.

There's power in simplicity. The writer Henry David Thoreau once noted, "A man is rich in proportion to the number of things he can afford to let alone." What I think he meant was that we tend to accumulate too many things and get involved in too many things. The complexity of life that this causes makes us poor in both money and time. When we simplify our lives, we gain wealth.

> There's power in simplicity.

In any case, you're going to have to schedule rest and protect your schedule if you're going to capture the life-giving power of honoring the Sabbath principle. Scheduling rest helps me in multiple ways. First, there are the natural, physical benefits of rest we've explored in some depth in the previous chapters. It "sharpens my ax" so that I'm far more effective and focused when I am working. Yet there is much more going on here. Being deliberate about honoring a Sabbath day of rest is an expression of my trust and faith in God. It's an acknowledgment that I am not my own source. It reminds me that God alone is the reason for any accomplishments or success I have experienced. All of this releases more of God's blessing and favor upon my life. Just as the land is designed to produce more fruit when it rests every seven years, so God designed us to be more fruit-ful when we physically rest one out of every seven days.

It's a regular reminder I truly need, even after all these years. As much as I would love to say that I naturally work from a deep awareness of my dependence on God all the time, I don't. It's easy for me to start thinking and acting as if it's all up to me.

My friend and fellow pastor, Brady Boyd, author of a wonderful book titled *Addicted to Busy: Recovery for the Rushed Soul*, said it this way in an interview about his book:

> By choosing the Sabbath, in other words, choosing a day dur-ing the week, it doesn't have to be Sunday, I am protesting and rebelling against this innate desire that I have to trust and to worship my self-sufficiency. So it's literally, Sabbath is a protest—I cannot do this on my own. I cannot do this by myself. So out of protest against my own self-sufficiency that I know I have and most of us have. This need to be self-sufficient. I am going to slow down. I'm going to be a son during that day, I'm not going to be a pastor, I'm not going to be a ministry leader, I'm not going to be whatever title you have. I'm going to lay that aside. On the Sabbath day, I am the son. He is the Father, He is the potter, I am the clay, He is the Father, I am His son, I'm going to get my identity back.[4]

We all have the same impulse that Brady describes here, the temp-tation to think in agreement with the words of a motivational writer

---

4. Brady Boyd and Chris Mavity, "Are You Addicted To Busy?," Ministry Labs, 2017, https://resources.churchcommunitybuilder.com/conversations/add icted-to-busy-brady-boyd.

from a bygone era: "If it is to be, it is up to me!" That's simply not true for the believer. In fact, Jesus flatly tells us, "Yes, I am the vine; you are the branches. Those who remain in me, and I in them, will produce much fruit. *For apart from me you can do nothing.*"[5] It's a reminder we need regularly. We're dependent. It's all Him. Without our connection to Jesus, we're not capable of doing anything of eternal value. And the very act of taking a Sabbath rest jolts us into remembrance of that truth. That's part of the power of a weekly Sabbath.

Without the regular reminder, I can easily be swept up in my daily activities. I become distracted. Don't you do the same thing? Sometimes I do this because I so enjoy the reward that comes from hard work. As I anticipate the thrill of accomplishment, I can feel my heart kick into overdrive. I want to plow through my days to get that payoff of being able to say to myself, to God, and the world, "Look what I did!" I'm quicker to recognize this internal shift into "works mode" than I used to be. I know that God doesn't need my work; He wants *me*. I also know that He isn't seated in heaven handing out "gold stars." He already stamped me with His approval in Jesus Christ through His Holy Spirit. A Sabbath gives you and me an opportunity to recalibrate our relationship with God and rediscover who we are in Him.

> He already stamped me with His approval in Jesus Christ through His Holy Spirit.

By observing the Sabbath, I declare, "You are God and I am not." God designed us to rest, enjoy Him, and receive from His unending supply of grace. The Sabbath is good for us. But observing it runs completely counter to the fallen human nature and to the prideful spirit of this age.

5. John 15:5 NLT

Common Questions

Whenever I teach on the principle of the Sabbath, I invariably get a handful of questions from people afterward. The most common of these I have already addressed. Namely, "Does my Sabbath have to be on Sunday? (Or Saturday as the seventh-day sticklers assert?)" You already know that the answer is no. The Sabbath principle is life not law. Whatever day of the week works best for your unique situation is the one you should choose. There's no power in any particular day. The power is in what happens in you and between you and God when you trust him enough to unplug and disengage for a day every week.

I also hear this question a lot: "What should I do on my Sabbath, Pastor Robert?" My short answer is: "Enjoy! Enjoy your life. Enjoy your heavenly Father. Enjoy your family." Unplug from work. Disconnect from the online world of email and social media (which may actually involve breaking an addiction). Beyond that, just do whatever refreshes you. Just be mindful of God and His goodness as you're doing it.

On one occasion after I'd delivered a teaching about the importance of the Sabbath principle, a man came up to me, leaned in close as if he was about to share a dark secret, and asked, "Um, is it okay if I play golf?" I understood the root of his question. It's easy to assume, especially if you grew up in a religious household, that if the Sabbath is "holy" to the Lord, then the only things permissible on that day would have to be overtly "religious" activities—pretty much nothing but Bible study, prayer, and psalm singing, maybe some Christian television. Check Netflix to see if they have *The Greatest Story Ever Told*, *The Ten Commandments*, or *The Robe*.

That's certainly the direction the rabbis and teachers of the Law took the concept of the Sabbath under Rabbinic Judaism. By the time Jesus came on the scene, honoring the Sabbath day had become almost completely focused on outward actions and not at all on inward devotion, joy, or delight. Yes, delight! (You'll recall that the Lord, through Isaiah, said, "call the Sabbath a delight...")[6] The fact is, drawing lines between what is "secular" and what is "sacred" is artificial. For the believer, everything is sacred. The earth is the Lord's and the fullness thereof. What sanctifies an activity is what's going on inside you as you're doing it—even playing golf.

So, I answered this man, "Of course! Enjoy!" Then I elaborated and qualified my statement: "As long as you're not neglecting your family with too much time away at the golf course, and as long as you're being financially responsible, yes, you can play golf on your Sabbath rest day." Beaming, he turned to his wife, who was standing back at a short distance, and said, "I can play golf!"

Motioning her over, I asked her, as I nodded my head toward her husband, "Does golf refresh him?"

"Oh, yes," she replied. "He's been too busy to get out much these days, but when he does, he comes back a different man!"

"Do you like that 'different man' that comes back? Would you like to see more of *that* guy?"

"Well, yes. I would. He's more relaxed and chipper."

So, I repeated to her what I told him. "Well, I'm not the Holy Spirit. You both should check with Him. But I think if it refreshes him, as long as he is not taking too much time away from you, and is financially responsible about it, I'd say he should enjoy his golf."

---

6. Isaiah 58:13

Then I added, "The key is, God wants you both to enjoy yourselves on your Sabbath."

At that point her eyes lit up, a mischievous smile crossed her face, and she said, "Oh, really? Then I can go shopping?" I laughed and said, "The same goes for you. As long as you're being financially responsible..."

If you enjoy golf, get out and play. But while you're out there on the course, thank God for the beauty of His creation. Commune with Him as well as with your playing partners. Whatever nourishes your soul and refreshes and invigorates your body...do it. Just do it *with* God. Make Him a part of your day, all day long.

> Make Him a part of your day, all day long.

That conversation leads us to another question I frequently hear whenever I teach about taking a weekly Sabbath rest: "What should I *not* do on the Sabbath?"

The short answer is, work. You should not do anything associated with your job, including checking email, unless absolutely necessary. Before the advent of mobile phones, we all had a work phone at work, and home phone at home. We rarely if ever received work-related calls at home unless it was an emergency. The home was a sanctuary, a refuge. Now all the barriers have been destroyed. The work-time versus home-time boundary line has been completely erased. Smartphones and an ever-present internet connection means we never actually leave the office. We drag it around with us wherever we go. Like Pavlov's famous dogs, we're conditioned to react instantly to whatever beep, chirp, or ding our phones emit to notify us of new texts and emails. Even in the middle of a family dinner or a deep conversation, the sound sends us reaching for our phones.

There is no way to truly, deeply rest at any level if we never disconnect. We must unplug from work if we're going to plug into the life-giving, soul-restoring, mind-sharpening presence of God.

For the same reasons, it is also vital to unplug from social media. Look, I'm on social media and use those platforms to encourage people and promote important things. But I am also very deliberate and firm about limiting my exposure to it through the week and I avoid it completely on my Sabbath. I've previously mentioned how our social media feeds have largely become a constant stream of negativity, anger, tragedy, and heartbreaking news. If what we read and see isn't making us want to punch someone, it's making us feel inferior and envious. (Of course, I know some of the things we read are good news about our friends or cute things from our family.) Even so, carrying around your smartphone has become a way to constantly stream toxic emotions directly into your soul. What's worse, it's addictive.

For all these reasons, I strongly recommend that you make your Sabbath an off-the-grid day. Pretend you're an Amish person for the day! Use as little technology as you can. Rediscover silence. No doubt, at first it will bother you. We've become so accustomed to being constantly bombarded by sound in the form of media we are actually uncomfortable when there's no background noise. Quiet seems wrong, somehow. It makes us mentally itchy. Yet quiet is exactly what you need, especially if you want to hear the voice of God. Your heavenly Father wants to speak with you, but He's not interested in trying to shout to be heard over the racket with which we incessantly surround ourselves.

One of the powerful and important aspects of a full day of unplugged, disconnected, undistracted Sabbath rest is that you can actually *hear* God. And oh, what extraordinary things He wants to say to you! He wants to impart identity, showing you who He really made you to be and what He put you on this earth to do through Him. He wants to speak direction, insight, instruction, wisdom, encouragement, and comfort. He wants to tell you great and mighty things that you do not know.[7] As I've mentioned, I consistently hear comments along the lines of: "I wish I could hear the voice of God as clearly as you do, Robert." May I tell you something? God is speaking. He wants you to hear His voice. And there is nothing in this world that will put you in a better position to hear what He's saying, than giving yourself the gift of a true, quiet, God-centered Sabbath.

> God is speaking. He wants you to hear His voice.

Again, don't get overly rigid or legalistic about any of this. God made the Sabbath to serve you, not the other way around. As I've said, I normally make Monday my Sabbath and I protect it as much as possible. But occasionally something will come up that absolutely requires me to be involved or traveling on a Monday. I simply shuffle my schedule that week and take my Sabbath on a different day. Those kinds of adjustments are necessary from time to time, but I keep them to a minimum.

Another question I often field is, "What about an emergency?" Jesus actually addressed this very matter. I'm paraphrasing, but on various occasions Jesus said: If your donkey or ox falls in a ditch on the Sabbath, help it out![8] If your farm animals are thirsty on

---

7. See Jeremiah 33:3
8. See Luke 14:5

145

the Sabbath, lead them away to water!⁹ On another occasion He summed it all up by basically saying: Hey guys, relax! It's okay to do good on the Sabbath!¹⁰ I usually jokingly add, "But if your ox falls in a ditch every week, you're a bad manager!" In other words, if you have emergencies every week at work that interrupt your Sabbath, then put some better processes in place so you can rest one day a week!

Use common sense. Listen to the Holy Spirit, because He will guide you. If you have an emergency—if someone calls you and says, "Your business is on fire!"—God doesn't expect you to say, "It's a Sabbath, call me tomorrow."

To sum up this overview of what a good, restful Sabbath day might look like, let's turn to the Word of God for a description. Here are some excerpts from the 95th psalm, a song about entering into God's rest:

Let us come presence before His with thanksgiving; Let us shout joyfully to Him with psalms. (v.2)

Oh come, let us worship and bow down; Let us kneel before the LORD our Maker. (v.6)

Clearly, worship is a key to entering into supernatural rest. Continuing in this psalm, note the special focus of verses seven through ten. These are the verses quoted by the author of Hebrews that we examined earlier, concerning the Israelites' refusal to enter into God's rest in the land of promise. They speak of God's desire that we rest:

9. See Luke 13:15
10. See Matthew 12:12

146

For He is our God, And we are the people of His pasture, And the sheep of His hand. Today, if you will hear His voice: "Do not harden your hearts, as in the rebellion, As in the day of trial in the wilderness, When your fathers tested Me; They tried Me, though they saw My work. For forty years I was grieved with that generation, And said, 'It is a people who go astray in their hearts, And they do not know My ways.'" (vv. 7–10)

God instituted the Sabbath as a day of rest so that, among other things, we could reflect on His goodness, faithfulness, and love. Doing that builds your faith and trust in Him, which in turn, makes you a more powerful, more peaceful believer.

It is a day to soften your heart and believe His promises. Look again at the promises of the Lord regarding the Sabbath—provision, abundance, refreshing, wisdom—and remember that He gave you this day as a gift. He invites you to experience His presence, to enjoy Him, and be refreshed in Him. Millions of believers take days off and experience no refreshing at all. A day off isn't necessarily a Sabbath any more than a vacation is necessarily a sabbatical.

As you know, that was me for several years when we first launched Gateway Church. I felt guilty about resting while my staff worked. I felt obligated to let work leak into my day. And I ended up thinking about work constantly. As a result, none of my four tanks got refilled to any significant degree on my day off. Yet that is what a proper Sabbath can and will do for you. It will restore you spiritually, physically, emotionally, and mentally. Let's examine a few ways you can make sure you allow that to happen.

Refilling Your Tanks

No two people are alike. Humans come in a wide range of personalities and temperaments. What energizes you may actually drain me. For example, introverts find time alone more energizing than do extroverts. Opposites do attract, and Debbie and I know several married couples made up of one big extrovert and one major introvert. If such a couple attends a social gathering like a friend's Christmas party, the extrovert will leave the event completely buzzing with energy and life. Meanwhile, the introvert will have enjoyed the evening, but leave utterly exhausted and drained. He or she will need a few hours alone to recover.

What fills your four tanks will almost certainly be a little different from what fills mine. But the following kinds of activities have helped me in each area, and will serve to give you a starting point for discovering what refreshes you. Here's how I fill my four tanks.

Your Spiritual Tank

This is the simplest and most universal of all the tanks. There are no personalities or temperaments when it comes to human spirits. We're all created with the same needs and wired to connect with God in essentially the same ways.

> We're all created with the same needs and wired to connect with God in essentially the same ways.

Simply spending time in prayer and in God's Word seems painfully obvious, yet it is the best way I know for us to fill our spiritual tanks. This time might include pondering and declaring out loud the promises of God. There is great power in this practice. When you declare the truth about God and His goodness out loud, you hear it; and in hearing it, faith and trust rise within you. Your born-again spirit responds. And it's not only you who hears it. The angels of God and demonic spirits hear your voice as well. The angels snap to attention and demons tremble.

Ask the Holy Spirit to direct you to passages of Scripture that apply to an area of weakness or struggle in your life. Meditate on and even memorize that portion of Scripture, repeating it, speaking it, and praying it over yourself and your household. If you battle fear and anxiety, the Spirit of God might point you to Second Timothy 1:7:

> For God has not given us a spirit of fear, but of power and of love and of a sound mind.

Or perhaps Philippians 4:6–7:

> Be anxious for nothing, but in everything by prayer and supplication, with thanksgiving, let your requests be made known to God; and the peace of God, which surpasses all understanding, will guard your hearts and minds through Christ Jesus.[11]

Study these or other verses in different translations. Sometimes a fresh translation can make a familiar passage come to life in new ways.

Prayer—the privilege of being able to converse and commune with the mighty Creator of the universe—is a tremendous privilege.

---

11. NASB

But you wouldn't know it to observe the lives of most Christians. For many believers, particularly those raised in church, prayer is an obligation. An *ought*. A joyless task that earns us points or credits with God. If a lot of Christians were gut-level honest, they'd admit they view prayer as something that's probably good for them but doesn't actually change anything. Like running on a treadmill, it does you some good, but you don't actually get anywhere.

What a tragedy this is. The privilege of prayer is the opportunity to do what Adam and Eve got to do in the Garden of Eden—to commune with their Creator and have a real relationship with Him. It's the privilege they forfeited when they rebelled and were driven out of the garden after the Fall. There is a reason the tapestry of the Jerusalem temple blocking access to the holy of holies was torn in two from top to bottom the moment Jesus died. That ripped "veil" testified that Jesus' death had opened the way for us to walk right into the presence of God. His broken body became the new doorway into intimate fellowship with God.

It's unthinkable that we would neglect this astonishing opportunity. Walking and talking with God in the cool of the day is exactly what the Sabbath is for! Pour out your heart. Share your hopes, your dreams, and your fears. Then listen. Stop talking and quiet your soul long enough for your heavenly Father to speak. His words are spirit and they are life![12] God is all-wise, all-knowing, unspeakably mighty, and unconditionally loving. And that God has already been to your future, working and preparing good things for you there.

> Stop talking and quiet your soul long enough for your heavenly Father to speak.

---

12. See John 6:63

Why on earth would you pass up an opportunity to hear what He wants to say to you each week?

In addition to prayer and the Word, fasting is another way you can refill your spiritual tank. As you'll recall, doing some sort of fast was on Steve Dulin's list of suggestions for a sabbatical. This spiritual discipline is specifically designed to fill our spiritual tank as we deny our physical needs. Fasting helps us recognize our spirit's connection with God's Spirit in new ways.

Please understand, I'm not suggesting that you have to fast every Sabbath. In fact, the Shabbat for observant Jews around the world is a day filled with good food (prepared in advance). But occasionally, especially when you're feeling particularly drained spiritually and under attack, the Spirit of God may speak to you about abstaining from food or at least certain kinds of food for the day. If you feel that nudge, do it. There's spiritual nourishment in it. You already know that I recommend fasting from the internet on your Sabbath day.

Finally, worshiping and praising God in song is a beautiful way for us to refill. Whether I am singing my own words to the Lord, or I am singing along to one of my favorite praise and worship albums, I always find a tremendous amount of strength and peace during worship. When I feel like it is difficult to quiet my mind, music helps me shift my focus and enter God's presence.

Your Physical Tank

When someone mentions being tired, or says they're "exhausted," we generally assume they're referring to their physical body. When our four tanks are running on empty, we usually feel the deficit in the physical tank first and most prominently. As I mentioned in the opening of this book, our modern Sabbath-less lifestyles are killing us physically. Even many of those who exercise regularly and try to eat right are still tired and/or sick all the time because their physical tanks are empty and never get replenished. It's because God designed our bodies for deep, regular rest.

In her book *Sacred Rest*, Dr. Saundra Dalton-Smith writes:

> None of us are at our best when depleted. Our bodies cannot fully function when they are in a constant fight for excellence, high-performance, maximum effectiveness, and optimal capacity. The effects of the fight will ultimately be known. It's time to transition from our daily hustle to daily hush. In the hush, tension releases and recovery begins…Which activities cause you to feel energized? What habits create a sense of calm and relaxation? Make an effort to find out what restores you.[13]

The Sabbath is a wonderful opportunity to discover what refills your physical tank. What true Sabbath rest for the body looks like will vary from person to person. For the person who does hard physical labor for a living, a nap may be the most beneficial thing. For someone who is stuck in an office cubical fifty hours each week, a hike through the forest, a trip to the gym, or even digging weeds out of the flower beds may be more restorative than lying around.

What replenishes you may change from week to week. Get to know yourself and be led by the Spirit of God. For me, sitting on the couch is rarely truly restful for me. Getting up and going for a walk is often the most invigorating thing I can do. On the other

---

13. Saundra Dalton-Smith, *Sacred Rest: Recover Your Life, Renew Your Energy, Restore Your Sanity* (New York: FaithWords, 2017), 40.

hand, sometimes the most prudent thing to do is take a nap or go to bed early enough to get a full night's sleep. We underestimate the power of regular and adequate sleep.

We are made of spirit, soul, and body, and we are designed to operate as one integrated whole. As it turns out, bodily exercise can sometimes feed all three parts of our being. I have a friend who loves to ride his bicycle. If it is a nice Saturday morning and he has a couple of hours to ride on the open road or on some local trails, then he is refueled in a big way. The physical exercise of riding his bicycle some-how unlocks his mind and heart. He communes with God, receives creative ideas, and returns home feeling like a new man!

> We are made of spirit, soul, and body, and we are designed to operate as one integrated whole.

All the things I have suggested are important ways to fill your physical tank, but the overall focus is to rest in Christ. Allow Him to show you what will recharge your body.

Your Emotional Tank

All three of my children are married and have children now. That means Debbie and I have a growing tribe of grandkids we enjoy immensely. Recently, our entire clan visited an aquarium. It was a huge delight to see our grandchildren encountering fish, sharks, and seals for the first time. Afterward we planned to all go out to eat. I asked my kids, "Okay guys, do you want to go to a burger place or a steak place? I'm buying." Well, I'm sure you can guess which option they chose! We all had a great time, and I went home after a very active day, feeling totally refreshed. In the words of counselor Gary Chapman in his perennial bestselling book, *The Five Love Languages,* "my love tank was full." Over the years, I've learned that being around family and friends refreshes me emotionally. What refreshes you may be something completely different.

I have a friend who is more of an introvert, who loves going to a big bookstore and just browsing the aisles alone. He may buy a book or he might not. There is just something about the activity of exploring the infinite world of books that feeds and nourishes something within him. His case demonstrates that emotional refilling doesn't have to cost a lot of money. Maybe a day strolling through antique or thrift stores fills your tank—even if you don't buy anything. Or maybe going to a park, museum, or art gallery gives you what you need. Ask the Lord to show you what will work for you.

> Ask the Lord to show you what will work for you.

At the same time, pay attention to those things that drain your emotional tank. At this point I need to repeat my warning about the internet and social media. Television news should be added to that list. All these types of media are likely to aggravate you, distress you, frighten you, or just make you sad. Every one of those emotions are a withdrawal, not a deposit, in your emotional tank. Aggravation, distress, fear, and sadness can never do anything but further deplete your already depleted emotional reserves.

When you're watching any kind of "entertainment" television, be mindful and aware of the kinds of emotions being created in you as you watch. Ask yourself, is your entertainment consistent with Paul's instructions to the Philippian church?

Finally, brethren, whatever things are true, whatever things
are noble, whatever things are just, whatever things are pure,
whatever things are lovely, whatever things are of good report,
if there is any virtue and if there is anything praiseworthy—
meditate on these things.[14]

Is the net effect of your media consumption throughout the week
draining your emotional tank? If so, I encourage you to submit this
area to the Lord and ask Him for other ways to be entertained that
do not work against your rest. And on your Sabbath, I continue
to advocate just unplugging from everything electronic. We need
quiet. We need to break addictions and dependencies.

I also suggest that you think analytically and prayerfully about
your relationships. Are there people and relationships that deplete
your emotional tank? There are toxic people in the world and they
tend to foster toxic relationships. Pray about limiting your exposure
to such people. If it's not possible to limit them, learn how to navigate
difficult relationships in order to protect your emotional health. The
Holy Spirit's guidance in this area is invaluable and always available.

Your Mental Tank

I mentioned in a previous chapter that I often read books on my
Sabbath that are completely unrelated to my work or calling. It's
too easy to mentally slip back over into work mode if I'm reading on
leadership or ministry. Soon I'm mentally applying what I'm reading to my challenges and opportunities, and the next thing I know,

14. Philippians 4:8

I'm stressed and trying to solve problems! In contrast, books in the genres of history, fiction, and adventure take me to places I've never been and nourish my mind. Invariably though, I'll learn or encounter something in those books that makes for a great sermon illustration or sparks a fresh way to attack a problem. But that's not why I'm reading. I'm reading for the sheer, invigorating joy of it. But the result is that it sharpens my mental ax.

I shared earlier about the first time I asked the Lord the question, "What replenishes me?" In time, He showed Debbie and me that one of the practices that refuels us most is to go to a quiet place where we can relax, read books, and sit on the porch in rocking chairs, acting like there is nothing in the world to worry about. Honestly, some of the best mental rest I receive is when I think about nothing. I spend time gazing into the distance and opening my mind to receive the thoughts of the Lord.

There is something wonderful about creating space to think—not strategically mull over problems or mentally rehearse upcoming conversations. Just . . . think.

> There is something wonderful about creating space to think.

Ask the Lord to inspire your imagination and let your mind wander. It's refreshing!

If you will make the Sabbath a priority and protect it—in the words of Isaiah, if you will make it your delight—God will meet you in that day in a powerful and refreshing way.

He will faithfully provide for you spiritually, physically, emotionally, and mentally if only you'll trust Him enough to just rest.

CHAPTER EIGHT

IT'S NOT ALL ABOUT YOU

The Christian needs to walk in peace, so no matter what happens they will be able to bear witness to a watching world.

—Henry Blackaby

It had already been a good three minutes since Rebecca pushed the button that shut off the engine of her car, yet she still sat behind the wheel in the driveway in front of her house. She was savoring a few moments of stillness and quiet, and bracing herself for what she knew was waiting for her on the other side of the door to her home. No, not violence or danger, nothing that dramatic. On the contrary, inside the house, eagerly anticipating her arrival, were a good husband, Zac, and three great kids, ages nine to thirteen. No, the only thing keeping her pinned to her car seat for that extra few minutes was the weight of responsibility.

Work. So much work. Rebecca couldn't remember when she didn't feel exhausted. She had been up and on the go for thirteen hours already and much remained to do before she could lay her head down.

This day was typical. Rising at 5:00 a.m., she quickly got ready so she and Zac could get the kids fed, ready, and off to school. A forty-five-minute commute each way in stop-and-go traffic bracketed a long, hectic day juggling deadlines and handling demanding clients. Now she would throw dinner together while Zac helped with homework and school projects. Eventually, after getting the kids bathed and into bed, they'd watch television for an hour while attending to work-related emails. Then they'd collapse, exhausted, into bed and prepare to do the same thing again tomorrow.

Zac's weekdays were no less demanding or draining than Rebecca's. He, too, endured a lengthy commute in nightmarish traffic to and from work. Between the lunatic drivers and frequent accidents that invariably seem to bring the flow of cars to a standstill, he commonly arrived at his job already fuming and tense. He arrived home the same way. In between those grueling drives, the job he used to love had increasingly become a drudgery. Aspects of it that used to excite and energize him now just stressed him out. His coworkers used to gravitate to him because of the positive, encouraging energy he exuded. No longer. Now, if anything, they tended to avoid him. Those who dared venture into his office immediately felt unwelcome.

The arrival of each new baby in their family had been a welcome cause for rejoicing. But each addition to their family also added to the financial weight Zac felt. At the same time, he felt guilty about the fact that Rebecca had to work outside the home. But neither one of them could see any alternative. He felt uptight and on edge all the time. He woke up frequently in the night stewing on things related to work or their needs as a family. This was his new normal.

The weekends brought no relief from the pace for either one of them. All three of the kids were involved in activities. Plus, the weekends were the only time they could address issues of repair or cleaning around the house and yard. As Christians, they were committed to being in church every Sunday as well. But lately the battle to get everyone out of bed, dressed, and in the car on time had turned Sunday mornings into the most stressful part of the week. Usually, by the time they got to church they all wanted to strangle each other.

For a while now, this kind of grim tension had seeped into every part of their home and lives. The strain on their marriage was obvious to both of them, but lately even their closest friends and relatives had begun to notice. So had the children. They had always been an affectionate and mutually honoring couple, but now they frequently snapped at each other. Neither felt the other was meeting their needs. At one time they had both been diligent to try to serve and please each other. Now, slowly, barely perceptibly, the exhausted husband and wife had grown to be more focused on their own unmet emotional and physical needs. The kids picked up on the simmering resentment this created, and it made them anxious and insecure. This resulted in either withdrawal or acting out.

Rebecca wondered how it had gotten to this point. There had been a time when she and Zac were shining examples of what it meant to be Christians. Their unshakable joy and peace made them living testaments to their coworkers and extended family of God's goodness.

> Their unshakable joy and peace made them living testaments.

Now neither one of them wanted anyone to know they were Christians, simply because they didn't want to be bad advertisements for Jesus.

"What's happened to us?" she whispered as she took a deep breath and reached for the car door handle.

Outward-Spreading Ripples

What happened to "Rebecca and Zac"—a composite of a lot of people I've known over the years rolled into one fictionalized couple—is that they were suffering from a severe case of Sabbath Deficiency Syndrome. In other words, they were chronically tired. They had each been running for too long on four near-empty tanks. They were living without margin.

What this story illustrates is that neither Zac nor Rebecca were the only ones impacted by their failure to understand the power and importance of Sabbath rest. Zac's perpetual exhaustion was hurting his wife. And Rebecca's was hurting him. As their marriage suffered, their kids did, too. Children can feel it when things aren't right between the parents. The lack of harmony and peace makes them fearful and less secure. Plus, both parents found themselves yelling at their children more instead of correcting, training, and nurturing them. If Zac and Rebecca don't begin to find the refreshing, renewing, refilling power of Sabbath rest, the trajectories of each child's life could be negatively impacted.

Like ripples from a stone dropped in a pond, the negative effects of their burnout and marginlessness impacted the marriage first, then their home, but soon radiated outward into all the other areas of their lives.

Their coworkers certainly noticed the gradual change. Many of the people Zac and Rebecca worked with had once been drawn to their peace and positivity. There had been a time when their teammates and supervisors noticed how they seemed to handle adversity and setbacks with a level of calm and grace that infused others with confidence. On more than one occasion, a coworker had privately come to them and asked, "What is it about you? There's something different." And that question gave them an opportunity to share their faith. They were no longer hearing that kind of question. Those within their circle of influence who knew they were believers were no longer curious about the difference Jesus might make in their own lives. It's a chilling thought, but it's very possible that the eternal destinies of numerous people were turning on the fact that these formerly vibrant believers were now chronically running on fumes.

At the same time, Zac and Rebecca's job performance had begun to suffer. Both had once been star performers for their respective employers. Now they struggled just to meet minimum acceptable standards. Brain fog, forgetfulness, fatigue, and a generally sour disposition all worked together to erode their hard-won reputations for excellence.

Ever outward the ripples radiated, even reaching into their futures. Although they couldn't have imagined it, chronic stress and weariness was compromising their health and actually shortening their life spans. God had planned for both to live long, productive lives in His service, impacting tens of thousands of people for the kingdom along the way. God's highest and best for them was to fulfill the promise of Psalm 91:16: "With long life I will satisfy him and show him my salvation." But unless they discover the power of Sabbath rest and trust God enough to enter into it, the terrible toll of living marginless, unrested lives will significantly shorten their time on this earth. And in the time they do have, their impact for the cause of Christ will be greatly diminished. Weariness was literally destroying their legacy and they didn't even know it.

> Sabbath rest is vitally important for you and your life, [and] it's just as important to those around you.

What this illustration brings home is that while Sabbath rest is vitally important for you and your life, it's just as important to those around you.

The more you discover about the kingdom of God, the more you learn that it's never all about you. If you're not resting regularly and deeply, you're not being the best person you can be. This, in turn, affects all areas of your life, everyone in your sphere of influence, and even eternity itself. It's that big a deal.

A Message to the World

God told the Israelites that the Sabbath was a sign and a message. It was a sign to future generations that they were a covenant people, belonging to God. It was a message to the world that this is a blessed people because they do things God's way. The same is true for you and me. Our honoring of the principle of the Sabbath sends a message to the people around us. It says, "I have a God who cares about me and takes care of me." But the positive effects and blessings of the Sabbath send a message, too. Your good, happy, peaceful life speaks. Remember what Jesus told his followers:

> I have a God who cares about me and takes care of me.

> "You are the light of the world. A city that is set on a hill cannot be hidden. Nor do they light a lamp and put it under a basket, but on a lampstand, and it gives light to all who are in the house. Let your light so shine before men, that they may see your good works and glorify your Father in heaven."[1]

It's true. Your life is speaking all the time. And even when you

---

1. Matthew 5:14–16

ignore God's wisdom concerning rest, and experience the same negative consequences that everyone in the world is experiencing, your life continues to speak. It's just not saying anything good about what it means to be in relationship with God. Jesus did *not* say: "Let your stress and weariness be so evident to other people that they want no part of the God you claim to serve."

Yes, honoring the Sabbath speaks to the world. And the supernatural power and blessings that come from honoring the Sabbath, speak to the world as well. One of the greatest testaments to that truth I've ever heard comes by way of a Christian-owned company during World War II.

Convictions Tested

"How many boats can you make in nineteen days?"

These were the words on the urgent telegram that landed on the desk of Ralph Meloon, president of Correct Craft, a small but growing ski boat manufacturing factory in Pine Castle, Florida, on February 9, 1945. The sender of the telegram was the US Army combat engineers, asking on behalf of General Dwight D. Eisenhower, Supreme Allied Commander of the Allied Expeditionary Forces battling Nazi Germany on the other side of the Atlantic.

General Eisenhower and his men had a pressing need. Ever since the successful D-Day invasion in June of the previous year, American and British forces had been fighting their way, yard by yard, across France. German forces had fought fiercely to hold every inch of ground, but had steadily been forced to retreat back toward Germany. By February of 1945, the Allies had liberated all of France, and German forces had retreated back across the Rhine river, which serves as the historic border between France and Germany. That meant that in order to defeat Germany, the Allies would now have to invade Germany. For the first time in the long, bloody war, German soldiers would be fighting on German soil, defending their homeland.

The invasion of Germany was code-named Operation Plunder and the military strategists knew it needed to happen quickly, for two reasons. First, the longer they waited, the more time it gave the Germans to dig in and prepare their defenses. Second, the Allied forces were rapidly running out of supplies and ammunition. It was now or perhaps never. A failure to defeat Germany completely would leave Hitler in power. We now know that would have left the thousands of Jews dying daily in the Nazi death camps helpless, with no hope of being liberated.

The invasion of Germany would require quickly moving tons of equipment and tens of thousands of men across the wide Rhine river. This task had fallen to the Army combat engineers, who now found themselves needing 569 "storm boats"—eight-man, high-speed assault boats with fifty-five-horsepower outboard motors that could quickly cross a river and beach at speed, thus allowing the soldiers on board to "storm" the other side. That's why Ralph Meloon's family's ski boat company and two other boat makers found themselves talking to Army engineers.

Correct Craft ordinarily turned out about forty-eight boats per month (roughly twelve boats per week, or two per day). But after praying about the request, the Meloon family committed their company to produce three hundred of the specialized crafts, and do so by February 28th. The Meloons made the commitment on February 10th. This would require hiring workers for extra shifts and running the production floor pretty much twenty-four hours a day. Even then, the goal seemed utterly unreachable. Right behind the telegram, the Corps of Engineers had dispatched expert production advisors to help the company quickly tool up for the seemingly impossible task. The message had arrived on a Friday. The decision to make the boats was made the next morning. There was not an hour to lose, yet they were immediately faced with a huge decision.

As committed Christians, the Meloon family had always closed the factory on Sunday. They didn't believe in working on the Lord's day and felt it was wrong to ask others to do so. They also shut down production for an hour or so each Wednesday for an employee chapel service, usually led by a local pastor. The government advisors told the Meloons that if they had any hope whatsoever of pulling off what they all were soon calling the "miracle production" goal, they would have to run the factory seven days a week. The calendar showed there were *three* Sundays in their tiny window of time to make three hundred boats. The loss of three productive days out of the handful they'd been given was unthinkable. But the Meloons understood something about the supernatural power of honoring the Sabbath day.

Looking back on the events a few years later, Ralph Meloon wrote:

> The question [of operating on Sunday] received only nominal consideration—we had settled that long ago with the Lord. "No," we intended to accomplish this task in such a way as to bring glory to God. God's plan for this boat company was not to work seven days a week. We made it known to the government representatives that we knew the job was impossible for man alone. We were setting out with faith that God would see us through, therefore we were attempting to do it God's

way. If they insisted on Sunday work, they should take the contract back.[2]

Please notice that Mr. Meloon obviously understood the very principles I'm sharing in this chapter—that the Sabbath is a key sign to a watching world. He saw his company's stand of faith concerning the Lord's day as an opportunity to demonstrate God's power and glory to skeptics and doubters. He just couldn't imagine that God would have them violate a core principle. So, he put God's promises to the test and God's reputation on the line. He assured the government representatives that, with God's help, they would hit their quota on time, but that they would not be running the factory on the Lord's day.

> The Sabbath is a key sign to a watching world.

Even so, the effort did not get off to an encouraging start. After closing the factory on that first Sunday, the number of boats they managed to complete on Monday totaled exactly...one. One boat. They now had fifteen days to make 299 more boats, and their current rate was one per day. On Tuesday, they tripled their production and made three boats. On Wednesday, they finished six more. They managed this even though the entire operation paused in the middle of the day on Wednesday to hold their usual midweek chapel service.

After three days of production, they had produced ten boats. Of course, they were still trying to get the workers for additional shifts hired and trained. Even so, the slow start sent Mr. Meloon and his extended family to their knees. They gathered in his home that

---

2. Ralph C. Meloon, Sr., "Miracle in Boats," *SUNDAY Magazine*, 1946.

night to pray and seek the Lord's wisdom. They didn't have to wait long for an answer. Mr. Meloon recalls:

> That very night my brother Walt was inspired to try a new machine and one change on the present jig.[3]

The new configuration of the existing equipment alone resulted in a big jump in output. A week later, production rates jumped once again when the new machine, conceived during the prayer gathering and hastily constructed, arrived. By February 19, one week after beginning their efforts, the pace of production had risen to forty-two boats a day. In that second week, it became clear to the government officials that, to their utter astonishment, Correct Craft was going to meet its target of three hundred boats ahead of schedule. And do so while shutting down each Sunday to rest and worship.

Remember the two other boat companies that had been contracted to fulfill the rest of General Eisenhower's request? They were falling behind, even though they were running three shifts, seven days per week. So, the government asked Mr. Meloon if his company could manage an additional one hundred boats by the deadline, upping their total to four hundred. He said yes, and they made it happen. In fact, the entire order was delivered ahead of time.

Over the next few weeks, The US military rushed more than seven hundred storm boats to eastern France to transport Allied troops across the Rhine river. However, on the eve of Operation Plunder, the army field commanders discovered that only the Correct Craft boats were correctly designed to accommodate the

---

3. Meloon, "Miracle in Boats."

outboard motors needed to power the boats across the river. More than three hundred of the boats could only be used as rowboats.

So, on the night of March 23, 1945, under cover of heavy artillery bombardment and close air support by the British Royal Air Force, the four hundred storm boats crafted only weeks earlier by Ralph Meloon's Sabbath-honoring workforce carried thousands of American soldiers into German territory.

The company was shortly thereafter awarded the Army-Navy "E" Award for excellence in production, and the press dubbed the manufacturing feat a "Miracle Production." It was indeed a miracle. Meloon would later write:

> For weeks people came from all over the United States to see the place where 400 boats were built in 15 days without infringing on the Lord's Day. To us, it was simply an indication that the Lord has again honored the obedience of His servants.[4]

After the war, the company grew and, through the decades that followed, launched or acquired a number of other boat brands. Today, Ralph Meloon's enterprise stands as the oldest family-owned water-craft builder in the world. The original company has expanded to include the brands Bass Cat, Bryant, Centurion, Nautique, SeaArk, Supreme, and Yar-Craft. Throughout the decades, the family has continued to run the business in alignment with biblical principles. As you may know, one of the Bible's many promises to those committed to doing things God's way is long life.[5]

---

4. Meloon, "Miracle in Boats."
5. See Deuteronomy 5:33 for example

On August 11, 2018, Ralph C. Meloon, Sr. passed away at the age of one hundred. A lifetime of doing things God's way, including honoring the principle of rest, resulted in a long, productive life. His obituary spoke of his home-going to heaven this way:

> He was surely accompanied by resounding trumpets and welcomed by loving relatives & friends who preceded him; many of whom found Jesus through his exemplary life & unwavering Biblical witness. He is survived by his wife of 81 years, Betty R. Meloon; three children, Marion L. Abel, Ralph C. Meloon, Jr, and Kenneth D. Meloon; nine grandchildren, twenty-six great-grandchildren and eight great-great-grandchildren.

Mr. Meloon knew what you and I need to understand. There is nothing quite like doing things God's way. In the busiest and most stressful times, God will bless your work when you go about it His way. Just as importantly, it will testify to a watching world that God is real, and He is faithful. Let's explore that truth in greater depth.

> In the busiest and most stressful times, God will bless your work when you go about it His way.

The World Is Watching (and Tasting)

The book of Matthew—in chapters five, six, and seven—presents, at length, one of Jesus' first sermons. We know it as the Sermon on the Mount. At the time the Lord delivered this message, he had only recently walked out of the desert after spending forty days there fasting and being tested. Yes, tested. Jesus, on your behalf and mine, passed the very same test that our ancestor, Adam, failed.

Adam and Eve, sinless and innocent, encountered Satan and fell for his deceptive temptation. Jesus, also sinless and innocent, encountered the same deceiver and the same lies, but sent him away frustrated. But there was a big difference between the two encounters, besides just the outcome.

Adam fell for a false promise in the midst of total abundance and comfort. God had placed them in the midst of an extravagant garden filled with every kind of fruit-bearing tree imaginable. The place was green, well watered, and lovely—a feast for all the senses. They were amply supplied in every way. In contrast, Jesus encountered the tempter in the middle of a barren desert at the end of a forty-day fast. Whereas Adam lacked nothing, Jesus lacked everything. Even so, Jesus remained faithful to God and to His mission. It's no accident that in two different New Testament books, the Apostle Paul explains that Jesus is "the Last Adam"—sent by God to undo the damage the first Adam had done.[6]

The first Adam, through his disobedience, unleashed both darkness and death (corruption and decay) upon the earth. From that time forward, darkness and death permeated everything. Then Jesus came.

With all this in mind, maybe it shouldn't surprise us to hear Jesus saying this to His followers in the Sermon on the Mount:

"You are the salt of the earth; but if the salt loses its flavor, how shall it be seasoned? It is then good for nothing but to be thrown out and trampled underfoot by men."[7]

---

6. See Romans 5:12–21; 1 Corinthians 15:20–28, 47–49
7. Matthew 5:13

In the next breath, Jesus says:

"You are the light of the world...Let your light so shine before men, that they may see your good works and glorify your Father in heaven."[8]

Jesus makes two declarations here concerning those who follow Him. (That's you and me, by the way.) You are "salt." And you are "light." Let's explore the implications of Jesus' two statements.

First of all, when He says, "you are salt," He clearly isn't suggesting that you're made out of sodium chloride, the name of the chemical compound we call salt. We all have a little salt in us, but it's not much. No, the Lord has something else in mind. You might not be aware of this, but salt is mentioned pretty frequently in the Bible, especially in the Old Testament.

For example, many people are quite surprised to learn that sacrifices and offerings under the Old Covenant were to be seasoned with salt. It's true! God commanded it in Leviticus:

"And every offering of your grain offering *you shall season with salt;* you shall not allow *the salt of the covenant* of your God to be lacking from your grain offering. *With all your offerings, you shall offer salt.*"[9] (emphasis added)

And in Numbers:

---

8. Matthew 5:14–16
9. Leviticus 2:13

"All the heave offerings of the holy things, which the children of Israel offer to the LORD, I have given to you and your sons and daughters with you as an ordinance forever; it is *a covenant of salt forever* before the LORD with you and your descendants with you."[10] (emphasis added)

Now keep in mind that everything God had the Israelites do in the Old Testament carried special meaning and symbolic significance. There are no insignificant details in the instructions God gave to Israel. Everything either pointed to Jesus or to what Jesus would establish in the New Covenant. So when we hear God say the "salt of the covenant" and the "covenant of salt" we should take notice. What's He pointing to here?

Well, for one thing, salt preserves. From the earliest days of human civilization, salt has been prized for its ability to preserve food. It causes things to endure. That makes it symbolic of eternity. It's no accident that God uses the word "forever" in conjunction with this command in the Numbers passage. He said, "It is a covenant of salt forever before the Lord." The point is that there is preservation power in being in covenant with God.

> There is preservation power in being in covenant with God.

Perhaps you've heard the term "the perseverance of the saints." That's a term that theologians came up with to describe the belief that those who are truly born again will persevere—in other words, *remain* saved. Well, this is related to that, yet different. This is about the *preservation* of the saints. God calls His relationship with Israel a

---

10. Numbers 18:19

"covenant of salt" because He's saying, "I'm going to preserve you." In fact, three times—twice in the Psalms and once in Proverbs—God says, "I preserve the souls of my saints."[11]

I find comfort in that. Don't you? We have three scriptural witnesses all testifying to the fact that God preserves us if we belong to Him. That tells me my connection to God isn't dependent upon *my* sticking power. It's dependent on God's covenantal faithfulness. Deuteronomy 7:9 tells us that "...the LORD your God is God; he is the faithful God, keeping his covenant of love to a thousand generations." And in the 105th psalm we read: "He remembers His covenant forever, the word which He commanded, for a thousand generations."[12]

Furthermore, God's preserving power isn't just for this present life. It's eternal. God preserves your soul forever. You're going to live forever because of the covenant you have with God through Jesus Christ.

That's why God commanded there be salt mingled with those Old Testament offerings and sacrifices. It symbolized preservation.

With that in mind, let's circle back to Jesus' statement in the Sermon on the Mount. Speaking to His followers, His disciples, He said, "You are the salt of the earth."

It may sound dramatic, but it's no exaggeration to say that God's people are preserving the world. Adam unleashed decay and death into the world, but our presence is keeping that decay at bay. The more Christians a society has, the less death and decay that society experiences. I've had the opportunity to travel to many remote parts of the world. I'm always struck when I go to a nation or culture

---

11. Psalm 31:23; Psalm 97:10; Proverbs 2:8
12. Psalm 105:8

where the gospel is relatively new or the Christian population is a very small minority. Death, oppression, injustice, and lawlessness are invariably so much more prevalent.

That's why our culture's rejection of Christian faith principles and morality is such a tragedy. The more our culture rejects, ostracizes, and bans Christianity in the public sphere, the more death and decay we'll see.

The good news is that here in the US, God's people are everywhere. We're in the classrooms, courtrooms, factory floors, and executive office suites. And everywhere we live and work, we're preserving, because we are salt. Jesus said so! As you'll recall, immediately after that, He said we're also something else: light! "You are the light of the world."

Of course, on more than one other occasion Jesus said He, Himself, was the light of the world. How can we reconcile that? Is He the light of the world, or are we? It makes perfect sense when you understand that, on this side of the cross, we are *in* Jesus and Jesus is *in* us. Isn't that precisely what He prayed for in what has come to be known as His High Priestly Prayer, in John 17? Just hours before being arrested and taken to the cross, Jesus prayed that He and His followers would be "one" just as He and the Father had been "one."

"I do not pray for these alone, but also for those who will believe in Me through their word; that they all may be one, as You, Father, are in Me, and I in You; that they also may be one in Us, that the world may believe that You sent Me."[13]

That is why we are the light of the world. The true light of the

---

13. John 17:20–21

world is in us, and we are, at the same time, in Him. The fact is, you and I are the only light this world has. As John 1:5 reminds us, darkness cannot overcome light. Light

> You and I are the only light this world has.

dispels darkness. And just as with our "salt" role on the earth, this means we are the answer to all the misery and ugliness that sin unleashed upon the earth in Adam's Fall.

We are salt and we are light. We preserve and we illuminate. We prevent corruption and dispel darkness. We make life taste better, and we show the way.

I can't help but notice that Jesus followed his salt and light pronouncement with a pair of warnings. Concerning salt, He said that if it loses its "savor," or saltiness, it's no longer good for anything but to be thrown out and trampled underfoot. Back in Jesus' day, that is precisely what they would do with salt that had gone bad and could no longer be used to preserve or flavor food. They would take it and throw it on footpaths to keep them from being overgrown with grasses. Plants can't grow in salty soil. Jesus' hearers knew exactly what He was talking about. They knew that unsalty salt would literally end up being trampled under people's feet!

Similarly, immediately after saying, "You are the light of the world," Jesus pointed out that it made no sense to light a lamp and then cover it up with a basket. No sane person would do that. On the contrary, Jesus pointed out that if you go to all the trouble to light a lamp, you place it in an elevated, highly visible place so its light can shine as far as possible.

In both cases, Jesus is saying that, as salt and light, your role is to preserve and illuminate. And if you're not doing that, you're failing at a fundamental reason God has you in this world.

Many things can keep a believer from shining. There are lots of possible reasons a Christian might lose their preserving impact within his or her zone of influence.

> Your role is to preserve and illuminate.

But I know one certain way: ignore the principle of the Sabbath. Consistently fail to rest. Trudge through your days burned-out, stressed-out, and exhausted. Become the joyless, powerless, peace-less, victory-less kind of Christian that Satan hopes you'll be, simply because your four tanks are perpetually empty.

Far too many believers are living their lives that way. Weariness has made them salt that has lost its savor. Marginlessness has hidden their light under a basket. And as a result, the world around them is a much more corrupt, darker place than it should be. What a tragedy.

Step Up by Stepping Away

Can you see now that it's not just about you? Do you understand that a refusal to rest and recharge doesn't just rob *you* of the good life God wants you to experience, it hurts the people you love the most—your spouse, your children, and your friends? It robs them of the wonderful, grace-filled version of you they need in their lives. Don't they deserve the best you? The rested you? In her book, *Sacred Rest*, Dr. Saundra Dalton-Smith had this in mind when she wrote:

> I never again want to bring the toxins of work life into the sanctuary of my home. I've made this a key part of my personal rest strategy. My home and my life are far from perfect,

but they are worth protecting from unrest…My husband will not become my dumping ground for today's disappointments. My kids will not be my venting wall. My family will reap the rewards of my head and my heart pointing the same direction.[14]

Yet as we've seen, it's not just your loved ones who need what you can only provide when you're rested and renewed. Like pond ripples radiating outward, your coworkers, and everyone you encounter as you walk through your days, can be positively impacted by the life of God within you. But only if you're willing to step up and step away to take regular time to refresh and recharge. The fact is, for some who cross your path, their eternal destinies actually hinge on encountering the rested version of you. There are those within your sphere of influence that may only be reached for Christ through the salt and light of you.

Yes, rest is a gift God asks you to give yourself. Yes, He wants you healthy, whole, and blessed. But it's not just about you.

---

14. Saundra Dalton-Smith, *Sacred Rest: Recover Your Life, Renew Your Energy, Restore Your Sanity* (New York: FaithWords, 2017), 205.

CHAPTER NINE

REST AND HUMILITY

Once more, never think that you can live to God by your
own power or strength; but always look to and rely on
him for assistance, yea, for all strength and grace.
—David Brainerd, Missionary

As we approach the end of this study, it's time to confront the giant
that stands between you and the lifestyle of life-changing rest God
wants you to enjoy.

As we've seen, there are many reasons Christians don't fully
incorporate the blessing of Sabbath rest into their lives. In fact,
it often seems like the whole world is conspiring to keep us busy,
stressed, distracted, and on the move. The culture doesn't want you
to rest. The enemy of your soul certainly doesn't want you to rest.
And often, *we* don't really want to rest.

We've already examined many of the forces that pull your mind
and heart away from regular, renewing relaxation with God. Greed
is one. We want to have more and be more, and we don't trust God
to increase us His way. Fear is also a significant one. What do we
tend to fear about resting?

- Falling behind
- Not getting everything done
- Not getting promoted or recognized
- Disappointing people
- Incurring the disapproval of others
- Being viewed as lazy

But even greed or fear take a backseat to one particular obstacle to enjoying true, full Sabbath rest that encompasses the whole you—body, soul, and spirit. The giant that stands between you and all the blessings of being in covenant with God is the oldest nemesis of all. It was at the root of man's first sin. It even caused Satan's fall from heaven as an archangel. And it was one of the three temptations with which Satan tried and failed to snare Jesus. I'm talking about pride.

That's right, the sin of pride is often the primary thing standing between God's people and the blessings of Sabbath rest. Embracing the rest of the Sabbath requires both a recognition that we are dependent upon God *and* a willingness to be dependent on Him. Pride will allow neither of these. Simply put, there is something deeply embedded in the fallen man that wants to say, "Look at me! I did this myself!" Ever since we were evicted from the garden, something in our orphan spirits has driven us to desperately grasp and scratch and claw and flail to feel significant. All of this results in constantly comparing ourselves to others.

In other words, we want *glory*. We want to be *glorified* in the eyes of others. This was Lucifer's catastrophic conceit. He wasn't satisfied with reflecting God's glory. He wanted the glory for Himself.

You will recall that in the previous chapter we saw how Jesus declared you and I are "the light of the world." Look with fresh eyes at the exhortation with which our Lord followed that statement:

Let your light so shine before men, that they may see your good works *and glorify your Father in heaven.*[1]

Do you see it? The life and light of God placed within us through the miracle of new birth is meant to bring glory to God, not ourselves. The blessings we enjoy, the achievements we accomplish, the good works we do—they're all to point people to our wonderful heavenly Father. God wants to bless us because He loves us, but also so people who don't know Him will want to! Unbelievers should look at our lives and say, "This person's relationship with God looks wonderful on them. They're happy, they have peace, they're blessed, and they make every place they go better. The God they belong to must be good. I want to know Him, too!"

> God wants to bless us because He loves us, but also so people who don't know Him will want to!

This is why God made such a big deal of the Sabbath for His Old Covenant people. You'll recall that it was to serve as a sign. The highway department places speed limit signs at regular intervals along the highway because all drivers need a periodic reminder of what the legal speed limit is. Similarly, the weekly Sabbath rest was a regular, recurring reminder that they were in covenantal dependence upon God—that they belonged to Him, and that He was their ultimate provider and caretaker, not their own cleverness and strength. The Sabbath was also a sign to foreigners. When strangers and neighbors would see the Israelites refraining from work one

---

1. Matthew 5:16

day each week, yet prospering, they would see a living testimony of God's goodness and faithfulness.

Again, the impulse within us to ignore all of that is pride. We want to feel like we did it. We want credit. We want at least some, if not all, of the *glory*. Yet as we're about to see, there is no place for that when it comes to being in covenant with God. In Isaiah 42:8 God says, "I am the Lord...and my glory I will not give to another."

When God says, "rest," He means rest.

Abram's Nap

Abram is about to consummate the biggest business deal of his life. Like many Bedouin chieftains roaming the near East around 2000 BC, he was a herdsman of livestock and a savvy trader. As such, he had negotiated more deals, arrangements, trades, and covenants than he could count in his eighty-plus years. But recently he had been unexpectedly approached by someone far different from anyone he had ever done business with before, with a proposition unlike any other.

Several years earlier, Abram received a surprise visit by the God of the universe, the Maker of heaven and earth. This was a surprise because Abram—having grown up in a place called Ur of the Chaldees, where the dominant religion was worship of a false moon god named Sīn—didn't even know this God existed. Yet God saw something in Abram's heart and character that made him the ideal choice for a particular proposition.

The proposition was this: God would make Abram a great nation, multiplying his offspring so as to rival the number of stars in the sky or grains of sand on the seashore. And also, through one of those descendants, all the nations of the earth would be blessed. That was quite an offer. So, what was Abram's side of this deal? His part was to believe. That's it. His end of the bargain was to believe that God would do what He'd promised to do. That happens to be the character trait that God had noticed about Abram in the first place—"Here is a man who will believe Me. I'll count that as covenantal righteousness." God said to Himself.

This promise of innumerable descendants is a particularly big deal for Abram, because he's already up in years yet childless. He and his wife Sarai have never been able to conceive. So what God is promising here is nothing short of an extraordinary miracle.

Now in this era, an agreement this monumental clearly required a covenant ceremony. And appropriately, God instructed Abram to gather the necessary elements for the ritual, giving him a shopping list: "Bring Me a three-year-old heifer, a three-year-old female goat, a three-year-old ram, a turtledove, and a young pigeon."[2] Abram, being very familiar with these solemn ceremonies, knew what was up. He had likely witnessed covenant cutting ceremonies and probably had participated in a few. These animals would all be killed and cut in half. Then the two halves of each animal would be separated and placed a short distance apart, all in a row, making what amounted to a pathway or aisle. Then the two covenanting parties would walk arm in arm down that aisle, professing their commitment, faithfulness, and loyalty to the agreement. In essence, the two parties were saying, "May what was done to these animals be done to me if I should ever violate this agreement."

As sunset approached on the appointed day of the ceremony,

---

2. Genesis 15:9

Abram had acquired and prepared all the animals, and had everything set up. He was ready and willing to walk between those pieces with his new covenant partner, but then things took an unexpected turn. God put Abram to sleep! As Genesis Chapter 15 tells us: "Now when the sun was going down, a deep sleep fell upon Abram..."[3] This is somewhat like the groom knocking the bride out just as they are about to say their vows.

Then, while Abram snoozed, the ceremony went ahead without him:

> And it came to pass, when the sun went down and it was dark, that behold, there appeared a smoking oven and a burning torch that passed between those pieces. On the same day the LORD made a covenant with Abram, saying: "To your descendants I have given this land, from the river of Egypt to the great river, the River Euphrates..."[4]

Two symbolic items passed through the pieces of the sacrificed animals to seal the covenant between God and Abram—a smoking oven and a burning torch. One item represented God in the agreement, while the other represented... well, a proxy. Someone stood in for Abram and made Himself the guarantor of Abram's side of the covenant. You see, a flawed, fallen, sinful human couldn't really enter

> Someone stood in for Abram and made Himself the guarantor of Abram's side of the covenant.

---

3. v. 12

4. Genesis 15:17, 18

into this intimate kind of covenant with a holy God on his own. He would have messed everything up. Abram discovered that his part in this whole thing was to believe and to *rest*. So important was the resting part that God put him to sleep!

If you know the rest of the story of Abram, you know that a few years later, his resting and believing got a little shaky as he waited on God to begin fulfilling His promise. He and his wife Sarai got unrestful, and started working to try to help God out. Abram's *work* resulted in Ishmael. In the centuries to come, Ishmael's descendants would multiply into a vast people. He is believed by many to be the father of all the Arab peoples of the world. We should not be surprised to see that Ishmael's descendants multiplied greatly. God had previously spoken His promise over Abram that his seed would be like the sand of the sea and the stars of heaven. That spoken blessing was out there and in effect, even though Ishmael wasn't what God had in mind. He was still Abram's offspring, and as a result, God's blessing of multiplication was on him. Even so, he was not the promised son whose descendant would one day bless the whole world. Abram had to go back to resting and trusting God to see the son of covenantal promise come to be born. He did, and the rest is redemptive history.

A Rest Remains

I think it's significant that God put Abram to sleep at the critical moment of entering into covenant with him. The Abrahamic Covenant was a forerunner of the type of amazing promise-filled covenant God would one day make with you and me. There is no way we sinful, fallen humans could enter into a covenant of promise with a pure and holy God. So, God sent us a proxy, His Son Jesus, to walk between the pieces for us. Yes, back during Abram's nap, that was the son of God standing in for him, walking side by side with God through those animal halves.

This wasn't the first time God had to put someone to sleep so He could bless him and fulfill a promise. You'll recall that in the opening chapters of Genesis, God told Adam that "It's not good for the Man to be alone."[5] This was the only part of all God's creation activity that He did not declare "good." In response, God tells Adam that He's going to make a suitable companion for him. To do that he causes a deep sleep to fall upon Adam. When he woke up, God's promise had been fulfilled. God didn't want Adam's help. The Hebrew word translated "deep sleep" in Genesis 2 is *tardemah*. Would it surprise you to learn that it's the very same word used in the original Hebrew to describe the sleep that fell upon Abram at his covenant ceremony with God?

When God is trying to do something that only He can do, our part is always to rest and trust. Yes, we must obey when God gives us an instruction. Abram had to obey God's directive to go get the animals necessary for the covenant ceremony. But when it comes to bringing about the results of God's covenant promises, God wants us in a posture of rest. Why? Because the glory belongs to Him!

> God is trying to do something that only He can do, our part is always to rest and trust.

The writer of Hebrews clearly had this very truth in mind when writing the passage that says, "There remains therefore a rest for the people of God...Let us therefore be diligent to enter that rest..."[6]

---

5. Genesis 2:18 MSG
6. Hebrews 4:9, 11

We've already visited this passage several times. Nevertheless, there is still more gold to be mined there, especially when it comes to understanding how to fully rest in the finished work of our covenant proxy, Jesus Christ.

It's helpful to remember that, as the title of the book suggests, "Hebrews" was written primarily to Jews in the first century who had recently embraced Jesus as Messiah and to Jews who were considering it. Overall, the book is a powerful presentation of how all of the Old Covenant types and shadows pointed to Jesus, and how Jesus was and is the fulfillment of the Law. In other words, Hebrews makes the case to Jewish people that the New Covenant in Jesus is superior in every way to the Old Covenant—with better promises and a better High Priest. In chapter three, the writer begins to warn his Jewish readers that they are facing a decision very similar to the one faced by their ancestors who were camped on the edge of the promised land.

He reminds them that an entire generation failed to enter the rest of settling in the Canaan. Citing the 95th psalm, he quotes God as saying:

> "Today when you hear his voice, don't harden your hearts as Israel did when they rebelled, when they tested me in the wilderness.
>
> There your ancestors tested and tried my patience, even though they saw my miracles for forty years.
>
> So I was angry with them, and I said, 'Their hearts always turn away from me. They refuse to do what I tell them.' So in my anger I took an oath: 'They will never enter my place of rest.'"[7]

---

7. Hebrews 3:7–11 NLT

The writer here is plainly, bluntly, urgently declaring that his readers are facing the same decision. They can believe the proclamation of the Word of God about Jesus, accept him, and enter into the restful promised land of new birth in the kingdom of God. Or through unbelief, they can be like that generation about which God declared, "They will never enter my place of rest." Chapter three closes with these words: "So we see that because of their unbelief they were not able to enter His rest." As I've said repeatedly throughout this book, embracing the principle of the Sabbath is a step of faith. It requires trust in God and childlike faith in both His power and His willingness to provide.

Yet there is another, very important dimension to the Sabbath. Like the truth about God's invitation to rest physically and mentally, it is very good news if we'll just receive it.

Shabbat-ing from Dead Works

Chapter four is a stern warning—particularly for the Jewish readers of this letter but for all people in all places—not to miss out on this new, ultimate promised land of rest that God was making available through faith in Jesus. He's pleading, "Dear Jewish brothers and sisters, please don't make the same mistake your forefathers in the wilderness made!"

> God's promise of entering his rest still stands, so we ought to tremble with fear that some of you might fail to experience it. For this good news—that God has prepared this rest—has been announced to us just as it was to them. But it did them no good because they didn't share the faith of those

who listened to God. For only we who believe can enter his rest.[8]

The writer then points out that the Sabbath rest was first modeled by God Himself at the close of His six-day flurry of creation activity. He then summarizes with a powerful declaration that we have already noted on more than one occasion, "There remains therefore a rest for the people of God."[9] What we haven't examined closely are the two explanatory verses that immediately follow that proclamation:

For he who has entered His rest has himself also *ceased from his works* as God did from His. Let us therefore be diligent to enter that rest, lest anyone fall according to the same example of disobedience.[10]

Look again at those verses and recall that the Hebrew word at the root of our word "Sabbath" is *shabbat*, which literally means "to cease." *Shabbat* is to stop. To quit. So the statement that God *ceased* from His works literally means God *shabbat*-ed. Keep that in mind.

Finally, after reminding us that God sees everything and knows everything, he closes the chapter with one of the most precious and comforting promises in all of Scripture:

Seeing then that we have a great High Priest who has passed through the heavens, Jesus the Son of God, let us hold fast

---

8. Hebrews 4:1–3 NLT
9. Hebrews 4:9
10. Hebrews 4:10–11.

our confession. For we do not have a High Priest who cannot sympathize with our weaknesses, but was in all points tempted as we are, yet without sin. Let us therefore come boldly to the throne of grace, that we may obtain mercy and find grace to help in time of need.[11]

Because God has both imputed and imparted Jesus' righteousness to us in the new birth, the heavenly throne we approach as believers isn't a throne of judgment. It isn't a throne of anger, wrath, or condemnation. No, when you engage your heavenly Father, you approach a "throne of grace." The gospel really is good news!

> When you engage your heavenly Father, you approach a "throne of grace."

The writer sums up this passage about finding "rest" in the new "promised land" of the New Covenant by saying that this truth is really a basic, foundational truth of the gospel. The opening words of Hebrews chapter six say:

Therefore, leaving the discussion of the *elementary principles* of Christ, let us go on to perfection, *not laying again the foundation of repentance from dead works* and of faith toward God...

What does the writer mean by "not laying again the foundation of repentance from dead works?" The key is understanding that He was speaking to Jewish people who all their lives had been taught they had to strive and struggle (work) to gain God's acceptance. As

---

11. Hebrews 4:14–16

we saw in the way Jesus was criticized for healing on the Sabbath, the rabbis, Pharisees, and teachers of Law had turned the purity of the Old Covenant faith into a crushing, burdensome striving (working) to merit God's acceptance and approval. The writer of Hebrews is saying that this new and better covenant is like the one Abram entered into with God. Although it sounds too good to be true, under this New Covenant, you're not going to work, earn, or merit your way into a relationship with God. You're going to have to go to sleep (rest) and let a proxy (Jesus) hold up your end of the deal.

In fact, trying to earn it or merit it on your own actually disqualifies you from entering into it. This is what the writer meant by "repentance from dead works." You have to repent of trying to work your way into a relationship with God. You have to cease (*shabbat*) your religious labors. Instead, you simply believe the good news and trust in Jesus' ability to hold up your side. This is spiritually possible because, as Paul repeatedly emphasizes in his letters, through new birth you are in Christ and Christ is in you. Both things are true at the same time. You get credit for Jesus' perfect fulfillment of the mankind side of our covenant with God because you're in Him and He is in you. You have become one with Jesus just as He prayed would happen in the High Priestly Prayer.

This is why the writer of Hebrews clearly and repeatedly warns his readers about failing to enter into the Sabbath rest that remains for the people of God. Let's review. Concerning the Sabbath rest— ceasing our futile efforts to qualify for God's acceptance—he says:

- Unbelief will keep you from entering into this rest (Hebrews 3:19)
- It's appropriate to be concerned that you haven't fully entered it (Hebrews 4:1)

- Entering this rest means you cease (shabbat) from your efforts just as God did from His (Hebrews 4:10)
- You need to be diligent to enter it (Hebrews 4:11)
- Repenting from dead works is a basic, foundational key to living the Christian life; as elementary as milk is for a baby (Hebrews 5:12–6:1)

So, entering into the blessings of the New Covenant means, in a sense, going to sleep and letting Jesus walk your side of the covenant for you. It also means that you grow fruitful as a believer the same way you became one in the first place—that is, by resting in Jesus' performance of the covenant's requirements. You humbly and gratefully enter it in a position of rest, and you remain in it in a position of rest.

Perhaps now you're beginning to understand why pride is a major obstacle to entering a lifestyle of Sabbath rest. Doing so requires humbling ourselves and admitting to ourselves and to God that we can't do it and the only part we play is to believe. Pride hates that. Pride wants to pay. Pride wants to earn. Pride wants to be able to compare itself to others, thump its chest, and say, "I did more than they did."

Entering the Sabbath rest of the Christian life means opening our hands to receive a free gift. As Paul wrote:

God saved you by his grace when you believed. And you can't take credit for this; it is a gift from God. Salvation is not a reward for the good things we have done, so none of us can boast about it. For we are God's masterpiece. He has created us anew in Christ Jesus, so we can do the good things [good works] he planned for us long ago.[12]

---

12. Ephesians 2:8–10 NLT

Have you ever given someone an extravagant gift because you cared about them and wanted to bless them, and they, instead of simply being grateful, started frantically trying to figure out how to pay you back? That's pride. Pride simply cannot relax, receive, and be thankful.

Now, the passage we just looked at mentioned "good works" that God long ago planned for us. So, what about good works? If God doesn't accept and embrace us based on our striving and efforts, where do these "good works" come in? Let's explore that question in view of this revelation about spiritual rest in Christ.

Good Works Flow *from* Your Connection

Yes, God wants us to literally, physically take a Sabbath pause one day each week to refill our four tanks. As we've seen throughout this study, it takes faith (belief) to do that. We've also seen that God rewards such faith with supernatural increase and provision. But as we're discovering in this chapter, fully embracing the principle of the Sabbath goes much deeper than that.

The passages we've been exploring here show us that at the spiritual level, Sabbath rest is an attitude of the heart that rests in Jesus' finished work on the cross. It's a posture that refrains from insulting the grace of God by trying to earn our place in God's family. It's a way of living and thinking that doesn't diminish the staggering price Jesus paid to be our proxy in the great New Covenant ceremony of the ages.

> Sabbath rest is an attitude of the heart that rests in Jesus' finished work on the cross.

So, what about good works? Didn't Jesus say to let the world see our good works so they'll glorify God? Didn't James say that faith without works is dead? Yes, and amen!

The key to understanding this is simply realizing that our good works don't *earn* us our connection to God. However, good works are a natural outgrowth of being connected to God. They flow organically from being in a life-giving relationship with Him. You don't qualify for becoming or remaining a child of God through any effort of your own. A gift is a gift. It can only be received. But once you become God's child, the most natural thing in the world is to begin to exhibit the characteristics of your Father.

> We don't do good works *for* our relationship to God, we do them *from* our relationship to Him.

In other words, we don't do good works *for* our relationship to God, we do them *from* our relationship to Him. This is exactly what Jesus had in view when He said this to His disciples:

> "I am the true vine, and My Father is the vinedresser...Abide in Me, and I in you. As the branch cannot bear fruit of itself, unless it abides in the vine, neither can you, unless you abide in Me. I am the vine, you are the branches. He who abides in Me, and I in him, bears much fruit; for without Me you can do nothing."[13]

Jesus' declaration makes it clear that we're not capable of bearing real, eternal fruit apart from our connection to Him. But as we

---

13. John 15:1, 4–5

"abide" in Him—that is, rest in His finished work on our behalf—
we naturally can't help but bear fruit. This is how we bring glory to
God as others see our good works. In fact, later in that same passage
Jesus said, "By this My Father is glorified, that you bear much fruit;
so you will be My disciples."[14]

Yes, good works are important and significant. True good works
bring glory to God, not to you, and only when they are the fruit
of abiding (resting) in Jesus. The moment you begin to view good
works as some sort of currency that you earn to buy favor, blessing,
acceptance, or love from God, you've abandoned your position of
Sabbath rest. You've given pride a foothold.

There remains a Sabbath rest for the people of God. Humble
yourself, and in childlike trust, receive that rest. Abide in that rest.
Thrive in that rest. Bear much fruit in that rest.

---

14. v.8

CHAPTER TEN

THE TIME IS NOW

Are you tired? Worn out? Burned out on religion? Come
to me. Get away with me and you'll recover your life.
I'll show you how to take a real rest. Walk with me and
work with me—watch how I do it. Learn the unforced
rhythms of grace.

—Matthew 11:28–29 (MSG)

The late W. Clement Stone's life stands as a remarkable rags-to-riches
story of the kind that Horatio Alger is famous for telling. Stone was
born in Chicago in 1902, and his father died when he was only
three, leaving his widowed mother deeply in debt. At the age of six
he began hawking newspapers on a South Side street corner to help
his mother supplement her income as a dressmaker.

Clearly born with an entrepreneurial streak, by the age of thirteen Stone owned his own newsstand. And at the ripe old age of
sixteen, he dropped out of high school, got that era's equivalent of
a GED, and moved to Detroit to sell casualty insurance. At the age
of twenty, he borrowed one hundred dollars and launched his own
life and casualty insurance company, calling it Combined Insurance Company of America. It thrived: it survived the stock mar-
ket crash of 1929 and the Great Depression, and ultimately became

a huge nationwide insurer. By 1979, the company's annual report revealed more than one billion dollars in assets.

Stone, the former child whiz at selling street corner newspapers and teenage insurance-sales phenomenon, built the success of his company on training his sales force well. He, along with his contemporary, Norman Vincent Peale, was a pioneer in understanding the power of a positive attitude. Employees at Combined Insurance were accustomed to greeting each other with the cheery question, "How's your PMA?" which was an acronym for "positive mental attitude." But perhaps the most powerful and effective thing Stone gave his salespeople was a simple key to overcoming procrastination.

He knew from personal experience that sales can be emotionally hard and frequently discouraging. He also knew that it was basically a numbers game. Knock on enough doors or make enough phone calls and the sales will take care of themselves. Every no simply brings you one step closer to your next yes. The challenge was to keep his sales force from putting off those difficult calls. Fear of rejection, stress, and discouragement will fuel procrastination. They make it easy to rationalize delay and dillydallying. Stone knew he needed a way to help his salespeople break through in the critical moment of indecision.

> Every no simply brings you one step closer to your next yes.

Stone eventually hit upon a remarkably simple idea. He had thousands of bronze coins created that had three short words deeply engraved on each side: "DO IT NOW."

Each salesperson was issued one of these coins the day he or she was hired. They were trained to keep it in their pockets at all times. And they learned quickly to never, ever be on the job without that coin. Whenever they felt themselves wavering about making a sales call or contacting a prospect, they were taught to reach into their pockets and feel the writing on that coin. That tactile point of contact would remind them of the words on the coin: "Do it now!" For whatever reason, this absurdly simple device had a powerful effect. For countless salespeople in a moment of wavering, a simple reach into the pocket would fill them with the resolve to dial that phone number or knock on that door. A highly motivated, remarkably efficient sales force became the key to Combined's remarkable growth. Stone passed away in 2002 at the age of one hundred. A few years later the company he'd founded as a kid with $100 was sold for $2.56 billion.

It is said that occasionally when one of the older, highly successful salespeople at Combined is talking to a group of new sales recruits, he or she will reach into their pocket and pull out their own bronze coin. Invariably, that coin would be shiny and smooth on both sides, with no trace of the writing that had once been deeply etched into the surface— evidence of countless critical moments of decision in which a small encouragement was all it took to defeat the enemy of procrastination.

Your Time to Decide

You too are in a moment of decision, right now, as you read these words. You've stuck with me through a winding biblical journey along which you've seen the clear evidence that God is inviting you, asking you, imploring you to join Him in Sabbath rest. Yet the choice is yours. God will not force you to rest, although, as I discovered, your mind and body eventually will. As we've seen, the Sabbath is a gift you give yourself.

It's possible that I've convinced you of the validity, power, and importance of the Sabbath principle. (I certainly hope so.) It's possible that you fully intend to incorporate the things I've presented...soon. With the best of intentions, you may be purposing in your heart to start taking a day off each week to refresh and recharge and connect with God...right after you get a few more things squared away, just one more project in the books. You just want to finish out this quarter with strong numbers. Two kids need braces and one car needs tires, but as soon as those things are paid for, you'll start unplugging for a day. Sure, you now realize that you're chronically running on four near-empty tanks but this just isn't a good time to start falling off the grid on a regular basis. You're up for a promotion. It would look irresponsible.

If these or any similar thoughts about Sabbath rest are in your mind right now, I have simple words from the Lord for you:

Do it. Now.

Let's lay aside the spiritual, supernatural aspects of this decision for just a moment and focus on the purely natural reasons to start a lifelong practice this week of taking a weekly Sabbath. Mountains of research and evidence suggest that you're simply not the best version of yourself when you're unrested. Remember Lincoln's wise words about sharpening the ax? You're less creative, less focused, less observant, less intuitive, less patient, less kind, less persuasive, and less appealing when your tanks are empty. Your judgment is impaired and you make poor decisions. Your efficiency plummets, so accomplishing everything takes longer than it should. And because you're more mistake-prone, you end up doing many things over again.

All of this and more is the hidden price of Sabbath Deficiency Syndrome. The great, hidden plague of our times is costing you so much more than you realize. You see, even if there were no God in heaven... if no loving, supernatural power was standing by to help and bless you...you'd *still* be better off embracing the Sabbath lifestyle.

But oh, my friend, there *is* a God in heaven. His miraculous power to bless, accelerate, expedite, increase, and multiply stands by to rush in wherever a heart of obedient faith and trust trigger its release. Those who honor the principle of the Sabbath find the wind of heaven at their backs. As Proverbs 10:22 reminds us, when you increase because of God's blessing upon your life, there is no sorrow added to that blessing. There is a flip side to that coin of truth. When

> Those who honor the principle of the Sabbath find the wind of heaven at their backs.

you try to bless yourself with your own efforts, you'll find lots of sorrow added to whatever wealth you manage to scrape up for yourself.

"Okay, Robert," you may be thinking, "I'm convinced. I want to start honoring the Sabbath. What now? What do I do with myself on my chosen Sabbath day?" The answer to that question is never the same for any two individuals, but there are some general truisms I'm happy to share.

Strategies for Four-Tank Sabbath Renewal

Let me start by reminding you that your objective in the Sabbath is rest. Not excitement. Not entertainment. And certainly not productivity. As a result, it's very possible that as you plan your day of rest, you'll have this thought: *That seems like it will be kind of boring.* You'll recall that in the chapter on sabbaticals and the principle of the *shmita*, we noted that boredom isn't such a bad thing, especially as you first begin to make Sabbath rest a part of your lifestyle. We're so accustomed to being busy, overstimulated, multitasking, and bombarded with input to all five senses every waking hour, that a few hours of quiet and stillness will seem...just wrong. The fact is, where deep rest is concerned, boredom is a feature, not a bug. Nevertheless, it will take some time to break your addiction to busyness and become comfortable with the slow, still environment that leads to renewal.

That is not to suggest that there is no place for entertainment or fun on the Sabbath. On the contrary, your strategy for enjoying and benefitting from this day of rest begins with understanding that you need to refill *all four* of your tanks—the physical, the mental, the emotional, and the spiritual. As I've already noted, I personally find that a funny movie or some good escapist fiction reading refills my mental tank. But I don't spend my entire Sabbath in front of the television, or with my nose in a book. I know I have four tanks that all need some attention. For example, I know that time with Debbie, my children, and now my grandchildren restores and renews me emotionally.

For my physical tank, a leisurely walk in the outdoors, weather permitting, carries remarkable power to refresh and renew. Notice that I didn't say, "forty hard minutes on a stair-climber or a treadmill." There's nothing wrong with vigorous exercise or having fitness goals. But your Sabbath is not a time for advancing your personal goals. "Achievement" is for the other six days each week. This day is about enjoyment, delight, and renewal. And there is something profoundly renewing about being out in nature. When we have green grass, trees, plants, and flowers around us, blue skies and puffy white clouds

> There is something profoundly renewing about being out in nature.

above us, fresh air in our lungs, and the sounds of birds in our ears, we recharge in intangible but powerful ways. On a warm spring or summer day, take your shoes and socks off and stand in lush green grass, with the sun on your face. Close your eyes and let your heart swell with gratitude to God for how wonderful a thing it is to be alive.

Alive! That's something I no longer take for granted. In April of 2018 I came within a hairbreadth of moving on to heaven. My wife and I were spending some time together out in a rural place we own about an hour and a half away from the city. It's pretty much out in the middle of nowhere. While we were there, I wasn't feeling well. Then, to my sweet wife's dismay, I collapsed. She immediately called an ambulance and when the paramedics arrived, they couldn't get a blood pressure reading from me and had difficulty locating a pulse. We would later discover that I had been bleeding internally from two different ruptured arteries and had lost roughly half of my blood volume.

The paramedics told my wife that I wouldn't survive the long ambulance ride to the nearest hospital so they radioed for an air ambulance helicopter instead. By the time I was ready to be loaded into the helicopter, I had regained consciousness. At that point, one of the first responders pulled Debbie aside and said, "You might want to get in there and say anything you want to say." The implication was that this might very possibly be our last opportunity to talk this side of eternity. In that moment, we both thought I was leaving this world, so we said our goodbyes. Yet I wasn't afraid or sad. On the contrary, I was flooded with an overwhelming sense of peace. Even so, my poor wife had to hold her phone up while I recorded some final words of blessing and encouragement to my children and grandchildren.

How grateful I am for the heroic efforts of those paramedics. Obviously, I survived, although I required two surgeries and spent four days in the ICU, and another four days in regular care. It took four to five months for my blood levels to recover and eight to nine months to fully recover my strength.

As I said, I'm happy and grateful to be alive, but not because I'm afraid of dying. I wasn't then, and I'm even less so now. I can't describe the overwhelming sense of peace I had in those critical moments. I knew

I was on the threshold of seeing my Savior and that moment would be the most wonderful of my existence. No, I'm happy because I get to continue having an impact here on earth on behalf of that Redeemer-King I was about to meet face-to-face, and because I get to spend more time with Debbie and watch my children and grandchildren as they begin to make their own unique marks for the kingdom of God.

The Sabbath is a time to pause and remember that it's good to be alive—that it's good to be a child of God on planet earth. To count our blessings and stoke the fire of gratitude for our generous heavenly Father. Life is good, even when it's hard. As First Timothy 6:17 says, "God has richly given all things to enjoy." That's how you renew and recharge yourself physically, mentally, and emotionally on your day of rest.

> Life is good, even when it's hard.

The next time you feel discouraged or under attack, take some time to be grateful. Grab pen and paper and start listing things you have for which to be thankful. You'll be amazed at how good it will make you feel. Ask the Spirit of God to help you find *your* best ways to rest and recharge. He'll show you! He will replenish your empty tanks and refresh you, body and soul.

But what about your spirit? The Sabbath offers you a powerful opportunity to fill this most important of tanks. Allow me to share some things I've learned about how to make sure that happens.

Filling Your Most Important Tank

Daily quiet time with God is a wonderful discipline to have. A daily season of talking with and worshipping your heavenly

Father—whether at the beginning of your day or the end of it—will help you keep your spiritual tank from ever running too low. I encourage the members of Gateway Church to find at least fifteen minutes each day for this.

However, there are things God wants to accomplish in you and through you that can never take place in a quick few minutes before you dash out the door to start your day. The true power of a Sabbath day of rest is time—time for you and the God who loves you, and gave His Son for you, to connect. It is vital to designate significant space in your day of rest for engaging with God. But what does that look like in practical terms? Here in closing, allow me to share four steps the Lord has used powerfully and consistently in my Sabbath time with Him.

1. Quiet your mind. (Shut out all voices but God's.)

Throughout the week, our minds tend be a whirlwind of competing thoughts and voices shouting for attention. Many of these provoke negative emotional responses within our souls—anxiousness, fear, anger, and worry, just to name a few. It's not unusual for the typical believer to walk around stirred up and tense all day long. Our near-constant connection to social media has only intensified and amplified that tendency. If you could see your soul—that is, your mind, will, and emotions—it might look like a body of water with white-capping waves churning and roiling the surface.

The first thing I do when I want to engage the Lord at a deep level is calm those waters. I silence the voices. In other words, I order my soul to be still. David, the psalmist and king, understood this. In Psalm 62:1 he writes, "Truly my soul silently waits for God. From Him comes my salvation." And in verse five of that same psalm he actually talks to his soul, giving it a command: "My soul, wait silently for God alone, for my expectation is from Him." When you're anxious, fretful, or agitated, your soul is talking a mile a minute. That's when you most need to hear the voice of the Lord, but often your soul just wants to keep chattering. Pretty much the entire 42nd psalm is David giving his troubled soul a good talking to:

Why are you cast down, O my soul?
And why are you disquieted within me?
Hope in God, for I shall yet praise Him
For the help of His countenance.[1]

You see, your soul thinks it's in charge. And for the period of your life before you were born again, it actually *was* in charge. Your spirit was dead or dormant, so your soul got to run the show. But once God made you spiritually alive in Jesus Christ, your born-again spirit became the rightful boss. Your soul, however, doesn't want to be told what to do. It will throw a fit like a little baby when it's not getting what it wants or needs. This is precisely why David wrote the following in Psalm 131:2:

Surely I have calmed and quieted my soul, like a weaned child with his mother; like a weaned child is my soul within me.

> Climb up in your heavenly Father's lap and be still.

When a child is still nursing, it tends to want to nurse whenever it is on its mother's lap. If the baby isn't getting what it wants, it becomes agitated, squirmy, and fussy. But once a child is weaned, he or she

---

1. Psalm 42:5

comes to the mother's lap only for comfort and rest. This is the imagery David invokes concerning his soul. The one thing that will calm your soul is to be held by God. Climb up in your heavenly Father's lap and be still.

2. Focus your mind. (Turn to God.)

Have you ever tried to think about nothing? It's not possible. You can't simply make your mind blank. So, once you've quieted your soul, it's vital to focus on something. Obviously, when your goal is to engage God, you must turn your focus toward Him.

The Lord once gave me an unforgettable and somewhat painful lesson in focusing on the wrong thing. Many years ago, I was preaching as a guest minister at a church, and frankly, their worship team wasn't very skilled. As the corporate singing portion of the service began, I immediately noticed that the lead vocalist was frequently off-key. Soon I noticed the instruments weren't synchronized and seemed to be playing different chords at slightly different times. These mistakes got my attention and got me listening for others. *The sound mix isn't very good either,* I recall thinking. Before I knew it, I was mentally cataloguing a list of flaws and inadequacies in the whole worship experience.

I remember thinking to myself, "Wow, they really need help in this area. This is not good at all. Who could possibly enter into worship with music like this?" In the very instant that question crossed my mind, I glanced around to see if I was the only one noticing this lack of technical excellence. Immediately my eyes fell upon a woman across the aisle with her hands raised heavenward and tears streaming down her face.

"She can," said the familiar, gentle voice of the Father. "You're standing here criticizing while she's worshipping Me."

Needless to say, I repented on the spot. "I'm so sorry, Lord. Forgive me."

As I thought about that incident later, I felt as if the Lord said to me, "Robert, you need to understand something. When a person sings, I don't hear the voice. I hear the heart. I'm not flesh and blood, I'm spirit. So, when you worship, I'm not listening to the physical sound waves caused by the vibrations of your voice. I'm hearing what your spirit is communicating. And when it's communicating love, gratitude, and worship, it's more beautiful to me than you can comprehend."

Which do you suppose God prefers? Someone who has a technically beautiful voice but whose heart is as cold and hard as stone? Or someone who sings off-key but from a heart filled with awe and thankfulness?

> One of the most powerful and transformative things you can focus on is the goodness of God.

Yes, we have to focus on something, and one of the most powerful and transformative things you can focus on is the goodness of God. I've already mentioned the power of gratitude and suggested writing down the things for which you're grateful. Well, as it turns out, filling your heart and mouth with gratitude, particularly songs of gratitude, is the perfect way to approach God. Once again, we can look to the psalmist David for confirmation. Psalm 100 says:

Make a joyful shout to the LORD, all you lands! Serve the LORD with gladness; come before His presence with singing. Know that the LORD, He is God; It is He who has made us, and not we ourselves; We are His people and the sheep of His pasture. Enter into His gates with thanksgiving, and into His courts with praise. Be thankful to Him, and bless His name.

For the LORD is good; His mercy is everlasting, and His truth endures to all generations.[2]

How do you enter God's presence? With singing! I was talking to the Lord about this one time and heard Him say, "Every day I give you a song, and that song is your key into My presence for that day." Now when I go to meet with the Lord, I begin by quieting my mind, I put my heart in a posture of gratitude, then I listen for the song God wants to give me. He invariably puts a song in my heart. Sometimes I even wake up with a worship song in my mind. For the rest of the day, that song is my key into God's presence.

God wants to give you a song for each Sabbath day with Him as well. You only have to listen for it. You can sing it out loud if you want to, but you don't have to. What's important is that you're focusing on Him. Singing to the Lord with thanksgiving turns your focus toward God. Music and worship represent a key element of your resting time with the Lord. Once you're in His presence, you're ready for the next step in communion with Him.

3. Pray your mind. (Talk to God.)

This next step is very simple. Just talk to God like you talk to anyone else. He is a person. He has a personality. "Prayer" is just a spiritual-ized term for talking to God. What should you talk about? What-ever is on your mind. Whatever concerns you. You don't have to pray for world peace or the missionaries in Uzbekistan, unless of course, that's on your heart. You don't have to pray for all the US senators by name, unless the Spirit of God puts it on your heart to do so.

---

2. Psalm 100:1–5

He's your Father. Talk about what's burdening you. You're never going to pray passionately until you pray about the things you're burdened about. It might be your spouse or your kids. It might be your job, business, or finances. It doesn't matter what it is, as long as it's authentically you.

If you follow this advice and begin to bring personal areas of your life before God, eventually you will hear one of Satan's biggest lies whispered in your mind. You'll have a thought along the lines of, *You're just being selfish.* As you begin to lift your concerns up to Him, the enemy will invariably come to you and say, "Wow, you sure are a selfish person. You pray a lot about your business and your finances." Or, "…your children." Or, "…your relationships." Whatever area it is that tends to burden you the most will be the focus of this accusation. The deceptive thing about that message is that, at first blush, it will actually sound *religiously* correct. After all, every Christian knows we're supposed to be more concerned about others than ourselves.

You see, the enemy of your soul is also the enemy of your intimate relationship with God. And he is an expert at using lofty, seemingly noble-sounding suggestions to undermine your connection to your heavenly Father. He quoted Scripture to Jesus about the angels catching Him if He should fall. Remember Judas's reaction to Mary anointing Jesus with precious oil in an act of worship and devotion? He tried to make her feel bad about it! He complained that the fragrant oil could have been sold for a large sum of money to help the poor. The Gospel writer makes sure we understand that Judas didn't care about the poor at all. But that was his religious-sounding rationale for opposing the precious, intimate worship moment Jesus was having with someone He loved.

When you hear that voice of accusation, here's what you need to say in response:

"Yes, I talk to God about my business because it's not really *my* business. It's His. I am not my own, for I've been bought with a price. (1 Corinthians 4:20) Because I belong to God, everything I control belongs to Him as well. I'm just a steward. So, yes, of course I'm going to talk to God about the business I'm running for Him. I'm going to discuss every detail of it with Him to seek His wisdom and ask for His blessing and favor. The same goes for every other aspect of my life— my household, my family, my relationships, my finances, and my future. If it concerns me, it concerns Him, because it all belongs to Him. I am only His steward!"

Don't ever be reluctant to bring your concerns to God, but especially during your time together on your Sabbath. Note carefully the words of Philippians 4:6:

> Don't ever be reluctant to bring your concerns to God.

Be anxious for nothing. In everything by prayer and supplication let your requests be made known to God.

Notice that it doesn't say to let everyone else's requests be made known to God. It says, "Let *your* requests be made known to God." We find the result of doing that in the very next verse:

And the peace of God, which surpasses all understanding, will guard your heart and mind through Christ Jesus.[3]

---

3. Philippians 4:7

In other words, Jesus will assign peace to stand at the door of your heart and mind with a shotgun, saying to worry, anxiety, and stress, "Nope. You're not getting in here."

After you (1) quiet your mind, (2) focus your mind, and (3) pray your mind, then what? The next step in this progressive Sabbath encounter with God is...

4. Renew your mind. (Let God talk to you.)

Yes, it's vital to say to God what you want and need to say. But it's even more important to allow Him to say what He wants and needs to say to you. Yes, God wants to speak to you—clearly and powerfully. In fact, hearing what God has to say to you is the key to change and growth. It's true!

> Yes, God wants to speak to you—clearly and powerfully.

I beseech you therefore, brethren, by the mercies of God, that you present your bodies a living sacrifice, holy, acceptable to God, which is your reasonable service. And do not be conformed to this world, but be transformed by the renewing of your mind, that you may prove what is that good and acceptable and perfect will of God.[4]

Renewing your mind—that is, replacing falsehood and deception with spiritual truth—changes you from the inside out. It will absolutely transform every area of your life. You do that by letting God speak to you! (And believing what He says, of course!)

---

4. Romans 12:1–2

God can and will speak to you a number of different ways, including using other people and the inward voice of the Holy Spirit, but the most fundamental and sure of these ways is to prayerfully engage God's Word, the Bible. When I open my Bible on my Sabbath rest day with a heart to hear God speak to me, I almost always do. Sometimes I receive instruction. Other times it's comfort, insight, strength, peace, or wisdom. Often when I feel I really need to hear from Him, I'll ask the Spirit of God to tell me where to turn and read.

I recall one such occasion that changed the entire course of my life. I can tell you the exact date: September 16, 1999.

I was spending a Sabbath day with God and, in the spirit of sharing my burdens and concerns with the Lord (step 3), I had been talking with Him about my future in ministry. I had been on staff at a wonderful church for several years, but I sensed that the time for whatever was next was growing closer. So, after that season of prayer, I grabbed my Bible and asked the Lord, "God, where do you want me to read?" Very clearly, I heard Him say, "Genesis 35 and Deuteronomy 11."

Naturally, I opened up to Genesis 35, a passage about Jacob struggling to figure out what was next for him in God's plan for his destiny. The first sentence of the chapter leaped out at me. It was as if the Spirit of God underlined it and used a yellow highlighter on it:

Then God said to Jacob, "Arise, go up to Bethel and dwell there; and make an altar there to God..."[5]

I knew that the place-name *Bethel* (Beth-el) means "House of

---

5. Genesis 35:1

God." As soon as I read that, the inner voice of the Holy Spirit immediately spoke to me and said, "I want you to move to Southlake and start a church—a house of God." Southlake at that time was a small suburb on the northern edge of the Dallas–Fort Worth metropolitan area.

As I kept reading, God began unfolding His plan for Gateway Church, including giving me the name! In reading about Jacob and Bethel, I was taken back a few chapters to an incident in which Jacob gave Bethel its name. In Genesis 28, Jacob was spending the night out in the countryside, sleeping out on the ground with a rock for a pillow. While asleep, he saw an extraordinary vision of angels ascending and descending between heaven and earth. When he woke up, Jacob said:

> "How fearful and awesome is this place! This is none other than the house of God, and this is the gateway to heaven."[6]

A place named "House of God" that was a "gateway to heaven." As I read that, everything inside me said, "Yes!" The Spirit of the Lord made it clear to me that the house of God I was to establish would be a place where many people would be saved and drawn closer to God—a literal gateway to heaven and heavenly things. Thus, Gateway Church was born. And the day it was conceived was a day I had set aside as a Sabbath!

> His inner voice is part of your birthright as a child of God.

God wants to speak to you, too. Hearing the voice of the Lord

---

6. Genesis 28:17 AMP

through His Word and through His inner voice is part of your birthright as a child of God. In John Chapter 16, just before Jesus went to the cross, He explained to His disciples that it was a good thing for Him to go away because He would then send the Holy Spirit to help them. In describing the Spirit's ministry, Jesus said:

> However, when He, the Spirit of truth, has come, *He will guide you into all truth*; for He will not speak on His own authority, but whatever He hears He will speak; *and He will tell you things to come.* He will glorify Me, for *He will take of what is Mine and declare it to you.*[7] (emphasis added)

What a wonderful, precious ministry the Holy Spirit has in your life. His assignment is to:

- Guide you into all truth
- Tell you things to come
- Declare to you what the Lord is thinking and doing

Does any of that interest you? Would you like to be steered into truth rather than believing lies or being deceived? Wouldn't you like to know what's ahead so you can pray, prepare, and plan accordingly? Don't you want to know God's will for your life? Of course, your answer is yes to all of this. Well, the Spirit of God is ready, willing, and more than able to fulfill His mission in your life. The only barrier is our busyness and the noise with which we constantly surround ourselves. It's not that God isn't

---

7. John 16:13,14

speaking, it's that we can't hear Him above the roar of our crazy, hurried lives.

That's the power of taking a true day of Sabbath rest every week. With intentionality and purpose, you create space to relax. You unplug from the electronic chatter. You get still. You calm the turbulent waters of your soul. You crawl up in your heavenly Father's lap and focus your full attention on Him with a heart of gratitude and expectancy. Then you attune your inner ear to His voice. That's an environment in which you can hear what God is saying.

RSVP

Two thousand years later, Jesus' gracious invitation still stands: "Come to Me, all you who labor and are heavy laden, and I will give you rest." At the opening of this chapter, I quoted this familiar passage from the lovely modern paraphrase, *The Message*. It bears repeating here:

> "Are you tired? Worn out? Burned out on religion? Come to me. Get away with me and you'll recover your life. I'll show you how to take a real rest. Walk with me and work with me—watch how I do it. Learn the unforced rhythms of grace. I won't lay anything heavy or ill-fitting on you. Keep company with me and you'll learn to live freely and lightly."[8]

"The unforced rhythms of grace..."

I like that, don't you? What an extraordinary invitation to receive

---

8. Matthew 11:28–30 MSG

from such a wonderful Savior. He is the nourishing, empowering Vine who says simply, "abide in Me and you'll bear much fruit." He is the Great Shepherd of the Sheep who leads us beside still waters and restores our souls. He is our Great High Priest who can sympathize with our weaknesses because He became one of us. He is the Living Water, who bids us come, drink, be refreshed, and never thirst again. This is the mighty, yet gentle Warrior-King who invites you to put your beeping, buzzing, chirping phone down once a week and walk with Him in the cool of the day, so He can tell you great and mighty things that you do not know. He is the one who, in Revelation 3:20 says, "Look! I stand at the door and knock. If you hear my voice and open the door, I will come in, and we will share a meal together as friends."

> He is the Living Water, who bids us come, drink, be refreshed, and never thirst again.

What will you say to His gracious invitation? How will you respond?

"I'm too busy"? "I've got too much going on"? Really?

Once during his earthly ministry, Jesus looked at a small group of people and said, "Follow me." Imagine it. The long-awaited Messiah, the Son of God, the Prince of Heaven, God in human flesh, inviting you to walk and talk with Him. To learn from Him. To partner with Him in ministry.

But one said, "Lord, let me *first* go and bury my father." In that day, burying a loved one was a yearlong process. First the body was anointed with fragrant waxes and oils, then placed on the shelf of a tomb until nothing was left but bones, which took at least a year. The fragrant anointings were to cover the smell of decomposition. Then the bones were gathered up and placed in a jar. That way many generations of family members could share a single tomb. This man was saying, "I'm responsible for tending to my dead father's body for several more months; when the process is complete, I'll come walk with you." Then, another said, "Lord, I will follow You, but let me *first* go and bid them farewell who are at my house."[9]

In other words, both answers were "Yes, but not right now." Both individuals were invited to come away with Jesus but put it off. Both had something they believed needed to be "first." Both had good intentions; the things they needed to accomplish "first" seemed so very important in the moment. They were wrong, and they missed the opportunity of the ages. Jesus has extended the same invitation to you that those busy men received. How will you respond?

May I tell you something? The secret to living the Christian life joyfully, abundantly, peacefully, powerfully, and fruitfully is a shockingly simple one: put God first. I promise you—more importantly, God's Word promises you—everything else takes care of itself when you do. Put Him first in your relationships, first in your finances, and first in your time.

> Put Him first in your relationships, first in your finances, and first in your time.

Dear friend, the Sabbath principle of rest is life, not law. It's an invitation, not an obligation. It's a gift, not an assignment. Open the gift. Start living. Accept the invitation.

When?

Do it now!

---

9. see Luke 9:57–62

ADDITIONAL COPYRIGHT INFORMATION

ABOUT THE AUTHOR

ROBERT MORRIS is the founding lead senior pastor of Gateway Church, a multicampus church in the Dallas–Fort Worth metroplex. Since it began in 2000, the church has grown to more than 39,000 active members. His television program is aired in over 190 countries, and his radio program, *Worship & the Word with Pastor Robert*, airs on more than 850 radio stations across America. He serves as chancellor of The King's University and is the bestselling author of numerous books, including *The Blessed Life*, *Truly Free*, *Frequency*, and *Beyond Blessed*. Robert and his wife, Debbie, have been married thirty-nine years and are blessed with one married daughter, two married sons, and nine grandchildren.